First Published in 1999

ISBN : 81-7479-021-7

Published by : Rakesh Goel
Kaveri Books
4697/5 -21A, Ansari Road,
New Delhi-110002 (India).

Tel. : 3288140 Fax : 011-7198902
e-mail : kaveri @ del 3. vsnl. net. in

Laser Typeset by : **Delite Printers,** Delhi-110035

PRINTED IN INDIA

Contents

Throughout this book Bombay and Madras have been referred to by their new names of Mumbai and Chennai respectively. Accordingly 'Mumbai Airport' refers to Bombay Airport and 'Chennai Airport' refers to Madras Airport.

List of Figures

Prelude

I quickly mount the steps of the narrow staircase leading to the tower. As I reach the tower landing a bit breathless with exertion, the sudden emergence into daylight from the semi-darkness of the staircase causes my eyes to shy away momentarily. I recover myself, enter the tower and glance at the clock on the strip of the wall above the huge glass windows. The digital clock is showing '0 2 3 0'.

No, not the Tower of London or the Eiffel Tower of Paris. It is the control tower of Mumbai Airport. The time is not 2 : 30 A.M or P.M but actually 8 0'clock in the morning; the clock has not stopped. It is indicating G M T—Greenwich Mean Time.*

My colleague, the controller whom I am to relieve is half sitting, half standing at the tower desk, with the headphones over his ears, his eyes darting from one side to the other listening and speaking out into the mike at turns as he handles the busy morning traffic. His hair is dishevelled, his voice hoarse and his eyes weary from a stretch of full night's work. The relief on his face when he spots me is evident.

*I go over to the monitor and scan through the list of current NOTAMs ** i.e messages conveying information regarding the current status of runways, taxiways, navigation aids, firing ranges and so on. While arriving I had already briefed myself at the meteolorogical office regarding the current and forecast weather. Then I move over to the tower desk, pick up the second head set and put it over my ears. I study the current traffic display—Air India 828 is on short final runway 27, Speedbird 851, Alitalia 763 and Indair 903 are all holding for take off; 15 miles behind Air India 828 is Jetair 405...*

---

* Actually U.T.C (Universal Coordinated Time)

** Short for 'Notice to Airmen'

As soon as I grasp the traffic situation I indicate my readiness to take over by mouthing a brief 'Okay".

My colleague nods and slowly removes his headphones and lets them hang around his neck. I step in where he leaves and continue the instructions—"Speedbird Eight Five One behind Air India Eight Two Eight on final line up runway two seven behind and wait—Jetair Four Zero Five continue approach report crossing outer marker". In between my colleague mouths a few words; 'Singapore 412 is delayed due bomb threat, is in isolation bay, Victor Golf Kilo returned after take off due engine trouble....' Even as I concentrate on handling the traffic, I digest the information given by my colleague and give a brief nod. He removes the headphones from his neck and hangs them on the peg. Slowly he goes behind me and picks up his bag, all the time keenly observing me and listening to my instructions. Change of watch is like handing over a baton in a relay race. It is a smooth and not an abrupt process. As soon as he feels that I am fully in the grasp of the situation, he shuffles off slowly.

I quickly get immersed in the handling of the traffic. Mornings are generally busy following a general pattern of departures in the early morning, building up to a peak traffic of mixed arrivals and departures by midmorning as the arrivals start to pour in from other places. The exchanges on the R/T—radio telephony—during peak traffic are continuous-listening to the aircraft as they report their positions, requests for clearances, coordinating with approach control and surface movement control on the intercom to fit the aircraft smoothly and expeditiously in the traffic stream and issuing clearances to aircraft in the clipped and monotonuous tone which is the trade talk of air traffic control which would be practically unintelligible to any one but the initiated. "Air India One One Two cleared to land wind two eight zero ten knots, Malaysian Two Four contact approach control one two seven nine, Victor Hotel Bravo hold south of the airfield standby to cross take off path runway two seven, Lufthansa Six Nine Three follow Singapore Airlines Boeing seven four seven ahead of you number two for departure...."

The traffic comes in a sort of wavelike pattern. At times there is an almost total lull. Rapidly the traffic builds up to a roaring peak with the R/T resounding with a babel of voices making it a tough task at times for a pilot to get a message through to the tower. Every participant in the game is fully keyed up with utter concentration.

Clearances are and can be given only once and have to be correctly understood and acted upon. No one utters a syllable more than necessary.

Suddenly the situation becomes taut with tension. I am in the midst of another wave of heavy traffic. There are four aircraft holding for departure and five in the approach sequence. Two other aircraft are requesting for start up. On final at 8 miles is Gulfair 823, Tristar. Number one for departure is a non-scheduled Boeing 737 call sign N1745K bound for Dacca. To expedite the traffic I decide to allow N1745K to take off before Gulfair 823 lands, making a quick judgement that being a B 737, a medium weight and highly manoeuverable aircaft it would be airborne and well off the runway before Gulfair 823 lands. I issue terse instructions to N1745K; "November One Seven Four Five Kilo, line up runway two seven and cleared for immediate departure". I stress the word 'immediate'. I ask Gulfair 823 to "Continue approach". N1745K acknowledges and enters the runway. While I expect the aircraft to commence roll and take off in one smooth motion without stopping on the runway (which is what is conveyed by the term 'immediate' in the clearance) it comes to a halt on the runway. I anxiously wait for the roll to commence—Gulfair 823 is coming closer. Still the Boeing 737 does not start rolling. I can see Gulfair 823 sinking slowly, wheels down. "Four miles"; I here the voice of the approach controller on the intercom. He is watching Gulfair 823 on his radar on the floor beneath and is warning me. Still N1745K does not start rolling. I decided to instruct N1745K to cancel the take off and instruct Gulfair 823 to "Go around" to avert a possible collision of Gulfair 823 ramming into N1745K on the runway or Gulfair 823 abandoning the approach on his own and pulling up and N1745K also taking off and both colliding with each other over the runway. At that instant N1745K starts rolling. It would be unwise to issue any instructions now, so I just watch. N1745K gathers speed and is airborne by about the middle of the runway and climbs steeply. I clear Gulfair 823 to land. He is just two miles from the runway. My professional training does not betray my tension. Gulfair 823 touches down and settles. "That was a close one", interjects the approach controller unhelpfully. I wipe the beads of sweat from my forehead which I know is not due to the warm weather.

The morning drags on. The time approaches 1:00 p.m. 0730 by the tower clock. A sense of relief floods me at the prospect of being relieved soon. I hear footsteps and know that my relief is on the way. Immediately his head pops in through the door.

I hand over to him in the same manner that I took over from the previous controller. I vacate my chair and move behind and wait and watch till he settles. Then with a cheery as well as weary 'Good day', I move out of the tower and start descending.

As I wend my way down the stairs, I ruminate; "What a way to earn a living!"

1

Initiation as Air Traffic Controller

After graduation in 1957 followed by a year's stint as a demonstrator at the Madras Christian College. I followed the customary next step of looking for a job. Those were the days when the major employer was the Government—jobs in industry were not many and mostly open to professionals like engineers and accountants. Jobs in the Central Government were favoured as they paid better than the State Government jobs. The Saturday UPSC (Union Public Service Commission) advertisements were the gateway to make an entry into the officer cadre of the Central Government. It was on the basis of one such advertisement that I applied for and was selected for the post of assistant aerodrome officer in the Civil Aviation Department. The process of recruitment was very simple. On the basis of applications received in response to the advertisement, a list of candidates about ten times the number of vacancies were called for an interview at Delhi. The interview board was chaired by one of the members of the UPSC and there were two other members, one from the Air Force and one from the Civil Aviation Department. No written test, no aptitude assessment.

Assistant aerodrome officer was the first level officer in the Directorate of Air-routes and Aerodromes of the Civil Aviation Department. The officers of this directorate comprised, at that time, sort of administrative and management cadre of the Civil Aviation Department. Their basic function was the provision of air traffic control services but they were also responsible for the administration and management of the aerodromes under control of the Civil Aviation Department. It was for this reason that they were never called air traffic control officers as in most parts of the world, but were called assistant aerodrome officers, aerodromes officers etc. which designation persisted till very recently though for the most part their duties had shrunk to provision of air traffic services only.

Newly recruited assistant aerodrome officers were required to undergo a training course of eight month's duration at the Civil Aviation Training Centre* at a place called Bamrauli near Allahabad. It was on account of this that I found myself on that cold November morning of 1958 reporting to the Superintendent of the Civil Aviation Training Centre.

The training at the CATC was for a period of eight months in those days-seven months of classroom training at the CATC and one month of familiarisation at one of the four international airports of Delhi, Mumbai, Calcutta or Chennai. The training was very rigorous and comprised subjects like air traffic control, navigation, fire fighting, theory of flight, legislation, administration. The main emphasis was of course on air traffic control, theory as well as practical. The practicals were conducted using a mock-up tower desk, with instructors taking the role of pilots, sitting in a separate cabin overlooking the mock-up tower desk from where they could observe the trainee working. It was a far cry from the present day Aerodrome Control Visual Simulators** which are in use for training in the advanced countries, which provide a simulated view of an airfield with aircraft landing and taking off. Still the simple simulator at the CATC did provide sound basic training.

The principal of the CATC at that time was Santokh Singh, a retired officer of the Indian Air Force. Many of the senior officers of the Air-routes and Aerodromes Directorate in those days were from the defence forces, mainly from the Navy and the Air Force.

---

* Redesignated as "Civil Aviation Training College" in 1990.

** An Aerodrome Control Visual Simulator was installed in CATC in 1991 but never put to use.

In those days the CATC imparted training not only to air traffic control officers but also to communication and technical officers of the Civil Aviations Department, as also to officers of the Aeronautical Inspection Directorate of the Civil Aviation Department. But the glamorous part of the CATC was the flying school where trainee pilots were imparted their initial training. However the Flying School was wound up sometime during 1965 or 1966.

Santokh Singh was an energetic and dynamic officer. He was a strict disciplinarian. He had us poor souls out every day at 6:00 in the morning in the bitter biting cold of Allahabad to do physical training. He ran a very lively training centre. The instructors were also dedicated and placed considerable demand on the students. One really had to labour hard to leave the portals of the CATC.

When I accepted that offer of appointment as assistant aerodrome officer, I had little inkling as to what I was letting myself in for. Like 98% of the population I had no idea of the work of an air traffic control officer. I believed the job to be a desk job and jobs being so scarce it did not even occur to me to think twice before accepting the job. Particularly as the starting emoluments of Rs. 315 per month were considered good those days (a lecturer's pay at that time was Rs. 196 per month at the bottom of the scale—this was of course prior to the introduction of University Grants Commission pay scales for teaching staff in universities). It came therefore as somewhat of an unpleasant surprise when I learnt of the type of work I had to perform. Still there was no going back; I had to go through it.

And so I completed my eight month's training in June 1959. I was posted at Chennai Airport and I reported to the Senior Aerodrome officer-in-charge of that Airport and assumed the office of Assistant Aerodrome Officer. On that day I had become an "air traffic controller" and while rising to higher positions in the course of my long service, remained basically an air traffic controller, till 31st May 1995 when I laid down office on retirement as Executive Director (Air Traffic Management) in the Headquarters of the Airports Authority of India at Delhi, which is the highest career position that an air traffic controller in India can attain.*

* The Court of Inquiry investigating into the mid-air collision that took place near Delhi on 12 November 1996, has observed in its report that the level of Executive Director as the highest post that an ATC professional can attain is not adequate. The Court of Inquiry has recommended that the Airports Authority of India (AAI) should have a Member (ATC) on the board to look after ATC matters.

2

Development of Flying and Air Traffic Control

The development of air traffic control is inextricably linked with the history and development of flying, as air traffic control is a function derived from the activity of flying. An account of the development of air traffic control would therefore need a brief discussion on the development of flying. Even in the early pioneering days of flying, starting from that day in May 1904 when Orville Wright made his first flight, some assistance was required from persons on the ground for these flights to be undertaken. The associates of the early pioneers in flying extended this assistance which consisted among other things of ensuring that curious bystanders and spectators did not come in the way of the aircraft. In those early days there were of course no formal aerodromes and rules to regulate flying. With the rapid progress in the subsequent few years in the technology of flying, when it became clear that it was not just a freak activity but a major development in the science of transportation, the world's first airfield, Port Aviation about 12 miles from Paris was completed in December 1908 and formally opened for business in May 1909. The United Kingdom got its first aerodrome at Shell-beach on the Isle of Sheppey, Kent in February 1909. With the air traffic still being sparse the need of a control tower does not appear to have been felt in the construction of these early aerodromes.

Very early in the history of flying it was realized that it was essential to end the basic hazard of the pilot's isolation by developing a communication system with the ground. And so we have it on record that the first wireless message from an aeroplane to a ground station 656 feet below was sent from a Curtiss biplane on 27 August 1910 by an American James Mccurdy. The message sent in morse code read; 'Another chapter in aerial achievement'. The first telephonic transmission from an aeroplane was sent by Lt. Paul W Beck on 21st January 1911. These were however of an experimental nature and it probably took some years before radio communication was employed on a regular basis for air ground communications.

During the period of ten years from 1910 to 1920 the technique of flying progressed rapidly. The system of licensing of pilots was instituted as early as in 1909. The English Channel was aerially conquered in the same year by Louis Bleriot who flew across the English Channel in 37 minutes and won a prize of 1000 £ from the 'DAILY MAIL'. He flew between 150 and 300 feet at a speed of 45 m.p.h without compass or watch. The next year, that is 1910, rudely witnessed the darker side of flying when the world's first mid-air collision took place. The first Trans-american flight was performed in 1911 by Calbraith P Rodgers which took 49 days to complete, covering a distance of 4321 miles with 69 stops. 1913 witnessed the first flight across the Mediterranean Sea from Cannes to Bizerta a distance of 470 miles. Britain's first scheduled air service was started in 1919 from Alexandra Park in North London to Blackpool. In the same year International Convention on Air Navigation was signed at a conference held under the auspices of the League of Nations. The system of aircraft registration based on five-letter call sign, which persists even today, was established in the same year.

With the rapid growth in flying and increase of traffic, the need was felt at the airfields to regulate the movement of aircraft to and fro from these airfields. And so starting from the twenties we have references to the establishment of control towers at aerodromes like Berlin Tempelhof Airport (1920), Croydon Airport, U.K (1921) ('the airport buildings are like army huts except for control tower which stands on tall stilts') and Le Bourget Airport France (1924) ('at the top of the tower an airport official with binoculars signals the approach of air planes and identifies the airlines to which they belong'). The control tower's concern appears to have been limited to regulating the landings and take-offs on the runway with the use of visual light signals. Interestingly with regard to Temple hof Airport, the officials performing the task of keeping a watch on aircraft arriving and departing are referred to as 'sharp eyed air traffic policemen'.

In the decade between 1910 and 1920, flying appears to have been generally attempted only during periods of good weather, and navigation done with the help of a magnetic compass and visual reference to the ground. Some elementary rules of the air appear to have developed in the interests of safety and orderly flying in these days, such as; when two aircraft are approaching head-on each shall turn to the right; or, all turns shall be made to the left when leaving or approaching an aerodrome and so on. The basic principle applied while flying was 'SEE AND BE SEEN'.

Starting from the twenties pilots appeared to have ventured into flying during periods of night. An experimental night flight was conducted during February 1923 from Croydon (London) to Bourget, France ('Pilot has given his positions by radio and used aviation lights to make his approach').

Efforts were also made during this period to overcome limitations placed on flying by the vagaries of weather. This took the form of effecting improvements in weather reporting and dissemination as well as developing instruments to aid in navigation. An international system of weather reporting was established in 1924 wherein the "whole of the English speaking world as well as whole of Western Europe" were linked. French engineers developed in 1925a system of guiding air planes by wireless'. This system which appears to have been the forerunner of what was later known as the non-directional beacon (NDB) enabled the pilot to work out his bearing.

However even during the decade from 1920 to 1930 air traffic control appears to have been localised to the airspace in the vicinity of aerodromes and no control appears to have been exercised in the en-route phase. Pilots generally had a free hand in choosing the route while flying from one place to another. Another mid-air collision took place in April 1922 between a Daimler Airways DH 18 from London to Paris and a Farman Goliath of the French Airlines Grands Express Aeriens from Paris to London while flying through a valley killing 7 persons. This disaster highlighted the need for one-way system for avoiding collisions between aircraft flying in opposite directions. A one way system was set up between Le Bourget aerodrome in France and Croydon aerodrome in U.K. in the year 1924.

By the early thirties commercial aviation services had become well established and a number of countries operated international services also. Radio telegraphy was widely used for air to ground communication and an international code of air traffic communications was formally established in April 1932. This code was (and is still) known as the 'Q' code as the codes comprised 3 letters all starting with the letter Q. The concept of 'controlled flights', 'Controlled airspaces' and clearances appear to have emerged during this time and Croydon Airport at London introduced its controlled zone scheme in November 1933.

A more sophisticated navigation aid called the radio range was first developed in the U.S.A. in the beginning of the thirties. This facility, which was in use till about the end of the sixties embodied a very interesting principle. It consisted of two loop antennas at pairs, at right angles to each other. One antenna also emitted an aural tone comprising a dash and a dot (— .) which is the morse code for the character 'N'. The other antenna also emitted an aural tone comprising a dot and a dash (. —) which is the morse code for the character 'A'. The transmissions were such that in some sectors only N could be heard and in other sectors only A could be heard; Midway between these sectors however the characters interleaved to produce a continues tone (fig 2.1). These four directions in which continuous tone was heard were suitable routes for flight of the aircraft. From 1933 such radio ranges were installed along several routes in Europe and USA for the en-route navigation guidance of the pilots.

By the middle of this decade provision of air traffic control service began to be extended gradually to cover the en-route phase of the flights also. The first airway traffic control centre started functioning during December 1935 at Newark, U.S.A. It was operated by the staff of Eastern Airlines, United Airlines, American Airlines and TWA.

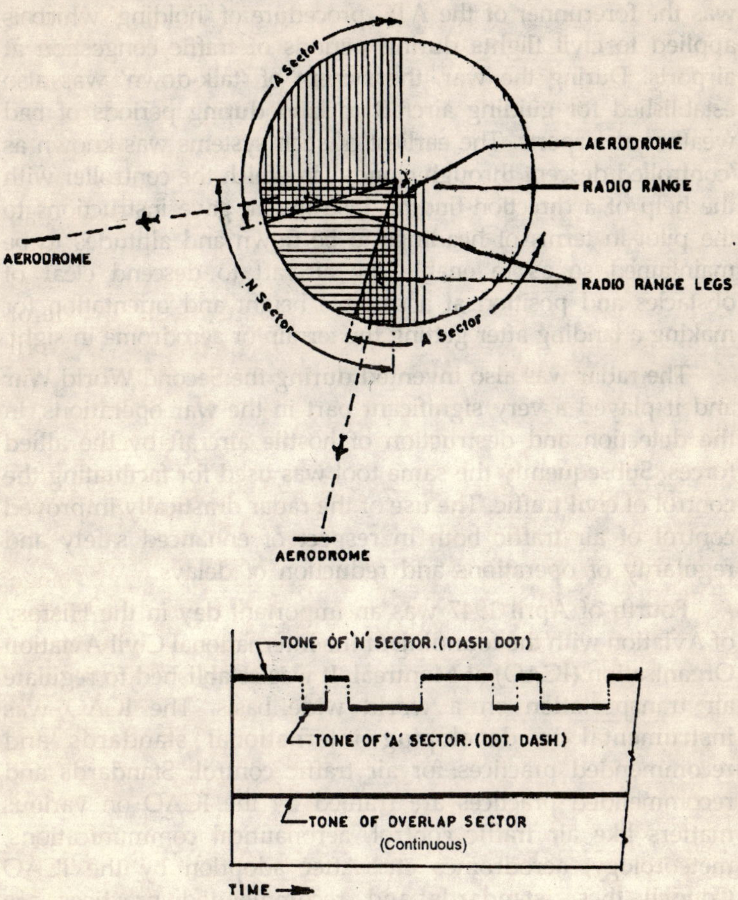

Fig. 2.1 : Radio Range

While air traffic expanded steadily in the subsequent years, it was the requirement to handle a very large number of aircraft during World War II that was instrumental for a rapid development of air traffic control techniques. Improved traffic control methods were necessitated because of a large number of aircraft returning to base at the same time. This necessitated the establishment of 'landing sequences' including procedure of 'stacking', that is directing aircraft to circle over the airfield at 1000 feet vertical intervals to consume time, while awaiting their turn to land. This was the forerunner of the ATC procedure of 'holding' which is applied to civil flights during periods of traffic congestion at airports. During the war, the system of 'talk-down' was also established for guiding aircraft to land during periods of bad weather at airports. The earliest of such systems was known as 'controlled descent through clouds', in which the controller with the help of a direction-finding instrument, gave instructions to the pilot in terms of headings to be flown and altitudes to be maintained so as to enable the aircraft to descend clear of obstacles and position at a suitable height and orientation for making a landing after getting the terrain or aerodrome in sight.

The radar was also invented during the Second World War and it played a very significant part in the war operations, in the detection and destruction of hostile aircraft by the allied forces. Subsequently the same tool was used for facilitating the control of civil traffic. The use of the radar drastically improved control of air traffic both in respect of enhanced safety and regularity of operations and reduction of delays.

Fourth of April 1947 was an important day in the History of Aviation with the founding of the International Civil Aviation Organisation (ICAO) at Montreal. It was established to regulate air transportation on a world wide basis. The ICAO was instrumental in developing international standards and recommended practices for air traffic control. Standards and recommended practices are framed by the ICAO on various matters like air traffic control, aeronautical communications, meteorology, aerodromes etc. After adoption by the ICAO Council these standards and recommended practices are published as 'Annexes'. Standards are requirements which each contracting state is bound to follow in regard to international aviation and in the event that any state desires to follow a different procedure, it is obligatory to file a difference with the ICAO. No such obligation is incident with regard to the Recommended Practices. ICAO also publishes other 'Documents' on various subjects designated by a four-figure number, which amplify and expand the basic Standards and Recommended Practices to help states in their implementation.

In so far as air traffic control is concerned, Annex-11, (Air Traffic Services) and Annex-2 (Rules of the Air) contain the relevant standards and recommended practices. The basic objectives of air traffic services were laid down in the 1st edition of Annex 11. The objectives of air traffic services as they stand today some fifty years later are almost identical word for word as in the 1st edition.

The objectives of air traffic services are listed in the box below :

Objectives of Air Traffic Services

1. **Prevent Collisions Between Aircraft.**
2. **Prevent Collisions Between Aircraft on the Manoeuvring Area and Obstructions on that Area.**
3. **Expedite and Maintain an Orderly Flow of Air Traffic.**
4. **Provide Advice and Information Useful for the Safe and Efficient Conduct of Flights.**
5. **Notify Appropriate Organizations Regarding Aircraft in Need of Search and Rescue Aid and Assist such Organizations as Required.**

As a guidance for practical implementation of air traffic control procedures, DOC 4444 Procedures for Air Navigation Services—Rules of the Air and Air Traffic Control (PANS-RAC) was published in the year 1950.* This document amplified, expanded and supplemented the basic standards and recommended practices set out in Annexes 11 & 2. The DOC 4444 is a comprehensive and amazing document. It is now in its thirteenth edition and has progressively expanded its scope over the years in step with the advances in aviation. It is verily the Bible of air traffic control and has been instrumental in standardising air traffic control procedures throughout the world.

How essential or even indispensible such standardisation of

* It was numbered as the 'Fourth Edition'. The earlier versions were published under a slightly different title.

air traffic control procedures are for the conduct of international aviation will become apparent when we consider a flight taking place say from Singapore to London. In the course of its flight lasting say about ten hours, the aircraft will cross more than a dozen countries each operating its own air traffic control system and it will also cross vast areas of oceanic airspace. The pilot of the aircraft has to communicate in turn with each of such air traffic control units, pass his estimates, request for and get his clearances. If every air traffic control communicated only in its own national language and had its own national procedures, it would just be impossible for such a flight to take place. However, with each nation following the standard ICAO procedures and communicating only in the ICAO 'official language' the pilots of various nationalities experience hardly any problem in communicating with the air traffic control centres and complying with the clearances. It may be mentioned here that ICAO has four official languages—English, French, Spanish and Russian.

ATC communication for international aviation can be done in any one of these four languages. However French and Spanish are used only in limited areas of the world and English is employed to an overwhelming extent. In order to ease further the problems that my arise due to the necessity of communicating in English for such of those pilots and controllers to whom English is not the mother tongue, ICAO has even standardised the phrases to be used in communication between pilots and controllers which is called standard phraseology. That is, the words and methods in which ATC clearances have to be given are also rigorously standardised. Even the pronunciation is to an extent standardised. For example 'ONE' is to be pronounced as 'WUN', 'NINE' as 'NINER', 'FIVE', as 'FIFE' and so on. From the beginning of their training itself the necessity of using the standard phraseology is impressed upon the controllers as the use of non-standard phraseology could and has in many cases actually led to ambiguity of understanding resulting in avoidable incidents and in some cases, even disasters.

As pointed out earlier, the standards and recommended practices are laid down by ICAO not only in regard to air traffic control but also in respect of all matters concerning conduct of international civil aviation like design and construction of international airports, provision of meteorological services, organisation of search and rescue and so on, each published under a different annex. At present there are 18 such annexes the last addition being Annex 18, Carriage of Dangerous Goods by Air.

With the establishment of the ICAO, airspace organisation on world wide basis for provision of air traffic services was brought into being. The airspace was divided into a number of flight information regions (FIRs), control areas and control zones with responsibility for provision of appropriate types of services within such FIRs, control areas and zones. The control areas and zones form part of the FIRs within which they are located. Within the FIRs, but outside the control areas and zones, responsibility rests for providing 'advice and information useful for safe and efficient conduct of flights', and for 'notifying appropriate authorities regarding aircraft in need of search and rescue aid' (Objectives 4 & 5 of Air Traffic Services). Within the control areas and zones in addition to the above, responsibility rests for prevention of collisions between aircraft, between aircraft and obstructions while operating on the ground and for maintaining an orderly flow of air traffic (Objectives 1, 2 & 3 of Air Traffic Services).

A system of air routes was also set up for proper channelisation of air traffic. Each route was designated by a combination of alpha-numeric characters.

A brief description of the Indian air space organisation comprising the various FIRs, Control Areas/Zones and Routes is given in Chapter 6.

With the steady increase in air traffic as well as advancements in aircraft design and technology in the period subsequent to World War II, more sophisticated navigation aids were progressively developed. These aids assisted the pilot for better navigation of his aircraft. Simultaneously they enabled more efficient provision of air traffic control. In the 'procedural' mode of control (described in the next chapter) the controller provides separation of aircraft based on the positions determined and reported by the pilots with reference to a navigation aid. The more accurate the navigation aid, the less is the uncertainity of the aircraft position and consequently less is the separation required.

Accordingly with greater sophistication in the development of navigation aids, lesser was the separation required between aircraft which was instrumental in cutting down delays.

It has been mentioned earlier that the NDB and radio ranges were the early navigation aids which were in use even earlier to World War II. In the period from the end of the war to 1960 more sophisticated navigation aids were developed which greatly facilitated flying as well as provision of air traffic control. The main aids that were brought into use during this period were the very high frequency omni-directional radio range (VOR), the distance measuring equipment (DME), the instrument landing system (ILS) and the secondary surveillance radar (SSR). They are briefly described here.

The VOR works on the principle of determining the bearing of an aircraft with respect to the VOR beacon by measuring the phase difference between two sets of beams transmitted by the VOR station. One antenna sends out waves that has the same intensity in all directions. A second antenna rotates and sends out a narrow beam of waves that when directed north coincides in phase with those of the first antenna. When the rotating beam is directed eastwards the two sets of waves are out of phase by 90° (1/4 of a wavelength). When it is directed south the phase difference is 180° and so on. A receiver in the aircraft measures the phase difference and displays the bearing of the VOR beacon along with the heading of the aircraft. The magnetic directions from the VOR are refered to as 'radials' i.e radial 180 means direction south from the VOR beacon and radial 045 means direction northeast from the VOR. The pilot could set his equipment to lock on and fly along any desired radial (Fig 2.2).

The VOR was more accurate than the NDB. However like the NDB the VOR indicated only the bearing of the aircraft and not its distance. This handicap was overcome with the invention of the distance measuring equipment (DME). In this system, the aircraft transmits radio pulses at one of a number of designated frequencies. Arrival of these pulses at a DME station located on the ground causes the DME station to respond to such pulses after a 50 microsecond delay on a different frequency. The time elapsed between the aircraft transmitting the pulse and reception

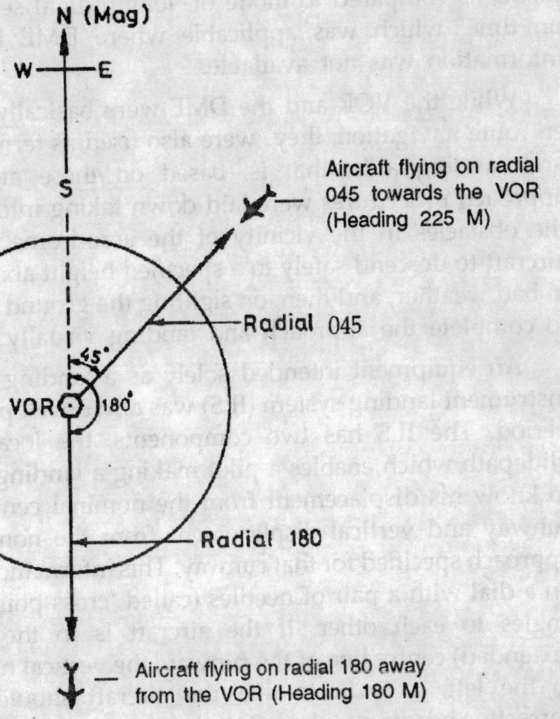

Fig. 2.2 : V.O.R. (Very High Frequency Omni Directional Radio Range)

of the responding pulse from the ground DME station is measured by a clock accurate to a few nano seconds and converted into distance which is displayed in digital form.

The position of an aircraft could therefore be established by combining the distance indicated by the DME with the direction as determined by a VOR, both located at the same place. The introduction of the DME was a boon to both ATC and pilots. DME distances are considered accurate upto 3 per cent of indicated distances for ATC purposes. The pilot could just read out his distance from an aerodrome and was spared the bother of having to plot the bearings from different aids to work out his position. ATC could use the distance information to apply a new kind of separation termed 'longitudinal separation based on distance' which drastically reduced the separation requirements as compared to mode of 'longitudinal separation based on time' which was applicable where DME based distance information was not available.

While the VOR and the DME were basically aids used for en route navigation, they were also used as terminal approach and landing aids; that is, based on these aids instrument approach procedures were laid down taking into consideration the obstacles in the vicinity of the aerodrome, to enable the aircraft to descend safely to a specified height above the airfield in bad weather, and then, on sighting the ground or the airfield, to complete the approach and landing visually.

An equipment intended solely as a landing air called the instrument landing system (ILS) was also developed during this period. The ILS has two components, the localizer and the glidepath which enables a pilot making a landing on a runway to know his displacement from the nominal centre line of the runway and vertical displacement from the nominal angle of approach specified for that runway. This information is displayed on a dial with a pair of needles (called 'cross pointers') at right angles to each other. If the aircraft is to the right of the (extended) centre line of the runway, the vertical needle swerves to the left, to indicate that the aircraft should be given a corrective heading to the left. If the aircraft is above the nominal glidepath, the horizontal needle moves down to indicate that the aircraft should descend faster to get back on the glidepath. In other words the pilot has to 'FOLLOW THE NEEDLE'. Later technology enabled the aircraft itself to get 'locked' on the ILS and carry out the approach automatically, that is the system itself corrects for any deviation from the centre line or specified angle of approach. While it is possible for the approach to be thus conducted automatically right upto the actual landing, in most cases the pilot takes over the control himself during the last stages of the approach and makes the landing visually.

An advanced version of the instrument landing system was developed in the eighties, the microwave landing system (MLS). This system has an 'azimuth guidance system' in place of the localizer and an 'elevation guidance system' in place of the glidepath. Its advantages over the ILS are many. It is less affected by terrain in its performance than the ILS. It allows the aircraft to make (multiple) curved approaches whereas the ILS permits only one straight approach the advantage is obvious; it will enable the aircraft to avoid hills or high terrain located directly in line with the runway. The MLS also facilitates approaches along any desired glide angle whereas in the ILS the angle of approach is fixed. Lastly the MLS can transmit limited information of aerodrome data which facility is not available in the ILS.

The ILS and MLS enable increased regularity as well as enhanced safety of operations.

The introduction of the secondary surveillance radar (SSR) in the later part of the fifties was another big step in the progressive development of air traffic control. The earlier version of the radar known as the primary surveillance radar (PSR) indicated the position of the aircraft in terms of bearing and distance from the radar antenna. It did not give information regarding the height of the aircraft. The SSR furnished information on the bearing, distance and also height of the aircraft.

A new type of navigation aid working on principles entirely different from the conventional aids described above came to be developed in the late sixties. This was called the inertial navigation system (INS). It was a 'self referenced' system termed as such on account of the fact that the system required for its operation, equipment to be carried only on the aircraft without need of complementary equipment on the ground. The system worked on the gyroscopic principle. A set of gyros carried on board the aircraft measured the accelerations to which the aircraft was subject in three dimensions in the course of its flight and a computer integrated these measurements of accelerations to calculate the displacement of the aircraft in three dimensions with respect to the initial location. The geographical coordinates of the initial position had to be accurately fed. The pilot could read his position in terms of geographical coordinates. The system did not therefore need any ground equipment for its functioning. It was also quite accurate though subject to some error over long periods of flight due lag, about 4 nautical miles per hour.

The positions derived from the INS could not be utilised to provide separation by the ATC as the DOC 4444 did not prescribe any separation standards based on that equipment.

The advent of the computer age found many applications in air traffic control. In the period prior to the employment of computer techniques, flight plan and movement data were manually processed by the air traffic control. Later, flight data processing systems (FDPS) and radar data processing systems (RDPS) enabled the rapid and accurate processing of vast amount of data that ATC had to contend with consequent upon the enormous growth of traffic in some regions. Functions like collision prediction, automatic despatch of movement and control data and so on helped the controller in the performance of his task. However the availability and use of such systems were limited to only a few regions where traffic volume was very high.

As mentioned in the beginning, air traffic control is a function derived from the activity of flying. Development of air traffic control has over the years kept step in step with developments in flying. The aspects of flying relevant to the exercise of air traffic control are mainly two—the volume of air traffic and the operational characteristics of the aircraft—that is the speed, manoeuvrability and like characteristics of the aircraft. Size, passenger capacity are less relevant for air traffic control. Of these two, the volume of air traffic has been showing a steady increase over the years and this increase is expected to be maintained in the future.

The operational characteristics of aircraft also changed much during the earlier years, that is from the end of the war to about 1970. The earlier reciprocating engined aircraft with speeds less than 240 kts gave way to the turbo-prop type of aircraft in the fifties with speeds reaching about 330 kts. They gave way to the turbo jets with speeds reaching 500 kts. The turbo prop and the turbo jet aircraft were sensitive from the fuel angle in that their consumption of fuel while on the ground was inordinately high as compared to operation at higher levels, unlike the reciprocating engined aircraft which were fuel-indifferent generally to altitudes. This difference in operational characteristic imposed a requirement on air traffic control to ensure by the issue of appropriate clearances that such aircraft were not unduly held on the ground or at low levels to avoid unnecessary fuel consumption. Then it appeared that the era of supersonic public transport would become a reality after the manufacture of the oncord as a joint British French Collaboration. This would have called for air traffic control to deal with traffic much faster and with climb and descent profile more complicated than the older generation of aircraft. However with the United States of America not approving the operation of supersonic public transport over its territory, the concept of supersonic public transport was aborted. For the last two decades the operational characteristics of public transport aircraft have not shown much change.

The volume of air traffic as mentioned already is on the increase. The present system of air traffic control it is generally agreed, would not be able to cope with the demands which the increase of traffic would place on it in the future. Keeping note of this, the ICAO has proposed a new system of air navigation as well as air traffic control based on the use of satellite technology. This system, known as the ICAO CNS ATM System is planned to be introduced in phases by the year 2010 AD. Chapter 8 gives a description of this new system.

3

Art of the Controller

The air traffic controllers' profession is an unique one. No other profession is really comparable to it. While it had its birth humbly as a sort of conveyor of information to the pilot from the ground on matters like weather conditions, state of the runway, presence of other aircraft and so on it had of necessity grown hand in hand with the technological advances in flying. Today it has emerged as a highly specialized profession and an inseparable part of flying. The air traffic controller does not merely convey information to the pilot on various matters affecting his flight; from the time that a pilot starts his engines till the time that he switches them off, the air traffic controller keeps a surveillance on the progress of the flight, giving positive and concise instructions at every stage of the flight to ensure that the flight goes off in an orderly and expeditious manner; that at no stage is there any possibility of collision with other aircraft or obstructions; that the best use is made of the airspace in the context of ever increasing traffic; that navigational assistance is given in areas of heavy traffic; that all possible assistance is extended in the event of an emergency, which includes not only contingencies like engine failure, but also events like lost position, hijacking (technically termed 'unlawful interference') bomb threat and so on.

The controller's relation in his professional life is almost exclusively with pilots of aircraft. The interaction in by way of radio communications. It is a nameless, faceless relationship effected only through 'voice' (and even that may cease in the future when 'data link' communications replace 'voice' as explained in Chapter -8.

Neither the pilot nor the controller have any personal identification. The pilot may be addressed as Speedbird 851, KLM 814 or Singapore 124, that is by the identification of the flight that he is operating at that time. The controller may be addressed as Calcutta control, Mumbai Radar or Delhi Tower depending on the place and unit he is handling at that time. Still, pilots operating regularly at airports do get familiar with the controllers' voices and sort of recognize them though they may never have met face to face. This aspect was very gracefully acknowledged by Mr. Rajiv Gandhi, late prime minister of India, who prior to entering politics was an accomplished airline pilot (of the Indian Airlines). At the inauguration function in 1984 of the Sixth Convention of the Air Traffic Controllers guild (India) of which he was the chief guest he opened his speech with the remarks "I may not know you by your faces, but I know you all by your voices."

The relationship between the pilots and controllers tend to be somewhat of an uneasy relationship. The air traffic controller nominally provides a 'service' to pilots of aircraft in the course of their flying, but the core of the controllers' function being prevention of collisions, he has perforce to regulate the movements of aircraft and in that process inevitably impose restrictions, conditions and requirements on the flight of aircraft which while essential for safety, is nevertheless frequently perceived as irksome by the pilots. The pilots perception of the role of air traffic control mainly depends on the pilot's general attitude and outlook coloured with his individual experience with air traffic control. The perception varies over a wide spectrum. I had carried out an exercise to elicit the views of their pilots on their perception of the role of ATC in flying giving them six possible descriptions of ATC. These were;

— ATC is inseparable from flying—A

— ATC is a great support to flying—B

— ATC provides assistance to flying—C

— ATC is a necessary evil in flying —D

— ATC is a nuisance to flying—E

— ATC is a positive impediment to flying —F

Most of the pilots who responded to the poll had either indicated 'A' (ATC is inseparable from flying) or 'B' (ATC is a great support to flying). The rest (and that very few) had given their perception as 'C' (ATC provides assistance to flying). Not a single pilot had given any of the other three options 'D', 'E' or 'F'. This clearly shows the very important role that ATC plays in the conduct of flying.

In my own reckoning, air traffic control, being as it were, a creature of flying, is in essence an institution to serve flying activities. At the same time in the interests of air safety which demands that the instructions of air traffic control be complied with by pilots without any resistance, it is necessary that ATC should be vested with sufficient authority for this purpose and so it partakes a function of a regulatory character. In the ultimate analysis ATC is both a service provider as well as a regulator, two somewhat contradictory roles. The opinion of individual pilots regarding the role of ATC is perhaps coloured as to how they view ATC-whether basically as a service body or a regulatory body.

What then is the part played by the controller in the business of flying ?

The controller's involvement with a flight commences actually even before the take off and ends only when the aircraft has reached its destination and has parked and shut off its engines. As soon as a flight plan (information concerning an intended flight) is filed, the air traffic control processes the same to see if it is in order. If not, ATC makes necessary changes or requests the pilot to make such changes as to make it acceptable. The flight plan is thereafter disseminated to all other air traffic control units under whose jurisdiction the flight may be operating.

The active part of air traffic control actually commences at the time of engine start up. The pilot has to obtain approval for starting up his engines, primarily in the context of traffic conditions. In the days of yore when piston engined aircraft were operating and traffic congestion had not assumed the character of a constraining factor, pilots just merrily started their engines and contacted air traffic control when they were ready to taxi out. But with the advent of turbined engined aircraft which consume disproportionately high amount of fuel on ground and at lower altitudes it had become inevitable to obtain start up approval from air traffic control so that aircraft after starting up, do not find themselves having to 'hold' for a considerable period awaiting their turn for take off. At many busy foreign airports, start-up time is actually stipulated in advance by ATC by allotment of what are termed slots. If the aircraft fails to take off within its stipulated slot it will find itself cooling its heels for a considerable time awaiting allotment of another slot.

After start up the pilot asks for 'taxi clearance'. This is authorization given by air traffic control to proceed on the ground up to the point of positioning for the take-off run. The controller specifies the route that the aircraft is to follow, depending upon the runway-in-use at that time, other traffic, suitability of the taxitracks for different types of aircraft and so on. The controller is responsible for ensuring that the aircraft while taxiing does not collide with other aircraft or non-permanent obstructions like vehicles etc. This aspect of the controllers job is particularly important as the pilot sitting in the cockpit is not afforded a good view of the ground close to the aircraft. The nose of the aircraft intrudes upon his foreward and sideward vision. It is quite possible that the pilot of a boeing 747 may not be able to see a small aircraft right under his wing. He literally cannot see beneath his nose'.

The next aspect of the controllers task is the control of the utilisation of the runways by departing and landing aircraft so as to ensure that there is no danger of collisions between such aircraft, while at the same time maintaining an expeditious flow of traffic. These are in a sense contradictory objectives as safety requires that the aircraft be kept well apart from one another while 'expedition' calls for crowding the aircraft so as to increase the rate of runway utilisation. This aspect of the controllers job is present in every facet of his work-reconciling the demands of safety with the requirements of expedition.

The ICAO DOC 4444 an amazing manual, which has progressively been developed over the years in the light of experience gained and new technological advances is verily the bible of the air traffic controller. It lays down the basic procedures applicable in the exercise of air traffic control. It stipulates the minimum separation applicable for various stages of flight required to ensure safety.

At this stage it is necessary to give an elucidation regarding two modes of air traffic control that are practised, radar control and non-radar control (which is less correctly but more frequently termed as 'procedural control'.) Under procedural control, which is generally applicable in areas where the controller has no means of knowing the position of the aircraft by means independent of the pilots' position reports, the decisions have perforce to be based on the information given by the pilot regarding his present and future positions. In the case of radar control, the controller is enabled to obtain continual and accurate information on the positions of various aircraft and his decisions are based on this information directly afforded to him. In view of this, the required minimum separation between aircraft is considerably less than under procedural control.

Under procedural control, in accordance with the procedures contained in DOC 4444, one can say that the maximum number of an equal mix of arrivals and departures that can be accomodated on a single runway, is about 25 in one hour. This is, assuming a scenario that works with clockwise precision which however is impossible to obtain in actuality. The actual number than can be handled in practice will be rather less. However with the help of radar which provides exact information on aircraft positions, more number of aircraft can be accomodated. At almost all busy airports like Heathrow (London) or JFK (New York) there are parallel runways one used for departures and the other for arrivals which help to achieve a smoother and more expeditious flow of air traffic. There are many busy airports still which handle both arrivals and departures on the same runway. Notable among them is Gatwick Airport in the United Kingdom.

With air traffic increasing over the years and pressurised by the need to accomodate more and more aircraft, many ATC administrations have progressively reduced the separation applicable between aircraft landing or taking off. The situation has become quite eerie at some aerodromes as a result of the same. At Sydney Airport in Australia for instance there are crossing runways and both are used at the same time with air traffic control adjusting the separation between flights so that they do not collide at the intersection of the runways. This kind of situation would have been unthinkable in the earlier years when either of the runways would only have been in use and even if they had been both used, they would for separation purposes treated as a singly runway; that is only after a take off or landing has been fully completed on one runway, a take off or landing would be allowed on the other runway. This is to give an adequate margin of safety to guard against situations where misjudgement on the part of the controller or unexpected manoeuvres by the pilot could result in danger of collision.

Air traffic control has, as it were, to meter out the departures and arrivals so that there is no danger of collision and at the same time endeavour to expedite the traffic. At busy airports during peak hours, it is a common sight to witness as many as ten or more aircraft 'holding' for their turn for take off. If a single runway is used for arrivals and departures the intermixing of landing and departing aircraft calls for quick thinking, sound judgement on the part of the controller as well as perfect understanding and coordination between different controllers.

The next aspect of the controllers job is the sorting out and separation of the aircraft that have taken off and are in the process of establishing on their track and other aircraft that are approaching to land at the aerodrome. This function is technically called 'approach control service'. This is a highly complex task and the complexity increases in geometric proportion to the number of aircraft handled. This is another feature common to all stages of air traffic control. Prevention of collisions is the core of the controllers responsibility; with two aircraft there is only one potential conflict, with three aircraft the possible conflicts will be three and with four aircraft the possible conflicts will be six and so on. In general if there are 'n' aircraft the maximum number of potential conflicts is $\frac{n(n-1)}{2}$. Each aircraft may not and does not in actual practice every time constitute a collision hazard to every other aircraft. The above is to illustrate the point that the load on the controller increases disproportionately to the number of aircraft handled.

Approach control may be effected either by procedural control or by radar control. The high density of traffic at important aerodromes makes it impossible to handle the traffic without radar. The minimum horizontal separation for radar control is five (nautical) miles which may be reduced to three miles under certain circumstances. In India at the few airports that radar is available, minimum radar separation of five miles is used; Whereas at busy airports in most of the developed countries, a minimum horizontal separation of three miles is employed. To the lay mind it might appear that a separation of three miles between two aircraft is a very comfortable situation. But translated in terms of time, separation of three miles between two aircraft, one following the other and each maintaining a speed of 480 knots. means a separation of less than half-a-minute-that is, the following aircraft will cross a point in less than half a minute after the preceding aircraft has crossed the same point. And if we imagine a string of aircraft like that it can well be appreciated that the situation is an awesome one requiring clock-work precision.

The progressive installation of radars at important airports where the volume of traffic warrants the expenditure on installation and maintenance of such radars, has led to replacement of procedural control by radar control. But at a majority of airports even now procedural control is used. Even at aerodromes where radar is available, procedural control has to be resorted to if there is a radar failure—a situation of frequent occurrence in India.

The essence of 'of separation' is that not more than one aircraft should be at the same place, at the same time and at the same level; one at least, of these three, should be different. But then how much difference is considered 'different'? These are specified in DOC 4444 are constitute the minimum separation standards mentioned earlier. For example the levels of two aircraft should be separated by a minimum of 1000 feet (330m) below FL 290 (29,000 feet) and by a minimum of 2000 feet (600m) above that level. This is termed vertical separation minima (VSM); or one aircraft should not cross a point traversed by a preceding aircraft flying at the same level on the same track within a period of less than 15 minutes; this is termed longitudinal separation based on time; or two aircraft should fly on tracks separated by a minimum of 15 degress when flying utilising a VOR. This is lateral separation illustrated in Fig. 3.1. Logitudinal separation and lateral separation together constitute 'horizontal separation'.

These separation standards are the criteria on which the controller bases his separation of aircraft. He has to ensure by the issue of appropriate 'clearances' that aircraft are separated in accordance with these separation standards and thereby present collisions while at the same time expedite and maintain an orderly flow of air traffic. A clearance is an authorization for an aircraft to proceed under conditions specified by air traffic control. Thus, 'CLEARED TO LAND', 'CLEARED FOR TAKE OFF', 'CLEARED FROM DELHI TO CALCUTTA VIA ROME FOUR SIX ZERO TO MAINTAIN FLIGHT LEVEL THREE THREE ZERO' are all examples of clearances. A pilot while flying in controlled airspace must operate his aircraft in accordance with the terms of the clearances. Any wilfil failure to act in accordance with such clearances will be considered an infraction of the law of the land. On the controllers' part it has to be ensured that the clearances issued do not result in the infraction of the miminum separation standards. Any such infraction is termed an 'air traffic incident' and is investigated to establish the causes thereof.

A few examples may be found interesting to show how the approach controller effects separation using the method of procedural control. This will illustrate the complexity of the task and the mental agility and keen mind that it calls for.

In the following examples the speed of the aircraft is expressed in 'knots' that is nautical miles per hour. A nautical mile is equal to 6080 feet. It is slightly longer than a conventional mile (statute mile), which is 5280 feet. Nautical mile is a measure of the distance subtended on the arc of the surface of the earth by an angle of 1 minute at the centre. As per ICAO regulations the speed of the aircraft may be expressed in terms of knots, kilometres per hour or mach number (ratio of the speed of the aircraft to the speed of sound), I have used 'knots' in my examples as this is the unit in which aircraft speeds are expressed in India.

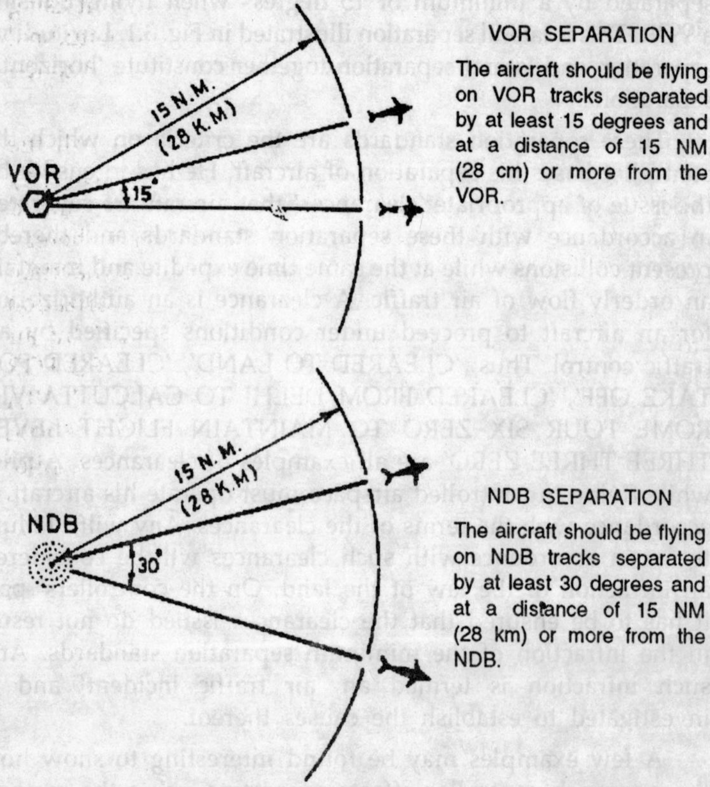

Fig. 3.1 : Separation Based on Navigation Aids

As regards the vertical position of an aircraft, this is expressed in terms of flight levels. This may be considered as denoting the altitude in hundreds of feet. Thus flight level 150 or FL 150 is *approximately* equal to an altitude of 15,000 feet. I stress the word 'approximately' as the actual altitude will differ from 15,000 feet. But this difference, for the purpose of our examples is only academic and technical and not material.

Imagine a hypothetical aerodrome called 'Hyperdrome' lying between two other aerodromes to its east and west called 'Eastdrome' and 'Westdrome' as shown in Figure 3.2 (a) Flights take place between Eastdrome/Westdrome to Hyperdrome and flights also take place between Eastdrome and Westdrome, overflying Hyperdrome. Hyperdrome is served by a VOR located at the aerodrome.

Now consider the following scenario :

Aircraft 'A' is on flight from Westdrome to Hyperdrome flying at FL 270 (27,000 feet) speed 480 kts (knots). Estimated time of arrival (ETA) Hyperdrome is 1000 (all taxiings in Greenwich Mean Time). Aircraft 'B' is taxiing for take off from Hyperdrome bound for Westdrome at time 0910. Filed FL 280 (28,000 feet). ATC estimates likely time of take off as 0920.

It is obvious that if B were to take off and proceed direct to westdrome, it will conflict with A as it will be crossing the level of A (FL 270—it is assumed that the two aerodromes are far apart so that A would have reached FL 270 at considerable distance from Hyperdrome) while climbing to FL 280. Restricting the level of B to FL 260 will not help as 'A' would have to descend from FL 270. So, the approach controller may resolve the conflict by clearing B to fly on VOR track 285 degrees, that is, different from that of A by 15 degrees (lateral separation) to climb to FL 280 and thereafter alter course for westdrome as shown in Fig. 3.2 (b). (For VOR based separation a minimum of 15 degrees is required.)

Let us now assume that in addition to A and B, another aircraft C is flying from Westdrome to Eastdrome *overflying* Hyperdrome at FL 250, speed 480 knots and estimating overhead Hyperdrome at time 0955, that is 5 minutes ahead of A. Fig. 3.3 (a) Now the problem is clear—A has to descend from FL 270 through the level of C at FL 250. What should the approach controller do?

In this case, the approach controller may clear A to 'establish' on radial 285 from Hyperdrome, and when so established, clear A to descend from FL 270. He can clear B to climb on radial 255 to FL 280 and then alter course for Westdrome as shown in Fig. 3.3 (b).

But as it often happens, the airspace to the south of the 270 radial from Hyperdrome may not be available on account of defence restrictions or some other reason. (In India approximately 35% of the land area comprises what are known as prohibited, restricted or danger areas which are not available or available only

ATC CLEARANCES (TWO AIRCRAFTS) [3.2 (a) & 3.2 (b)]

TRAFFIC : 'A' arriving Hyperdrome from Westdrome Flight Level 270 Estimated Time of Arrival Hyperdrome 1000 Speed 480 knots.

'B' departing Hyperdrome for Westdrome Estimated Time of Departure 0920

Flight Level 280

Speed 480 knots

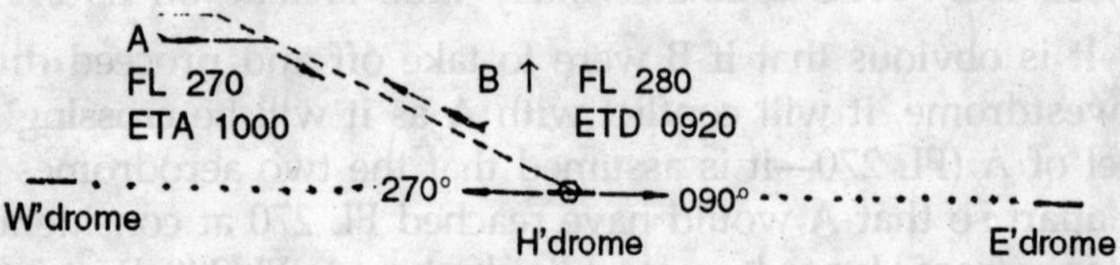

Fig. 3.2 (a)

CLEARANCES : 'A' to continue on 270 radial of Hyperdrome VOR and descend for landing

'B' to climb on 285 radial of Hyperdrome VOR to flight level 280; Regain track on reaching flight level 280.

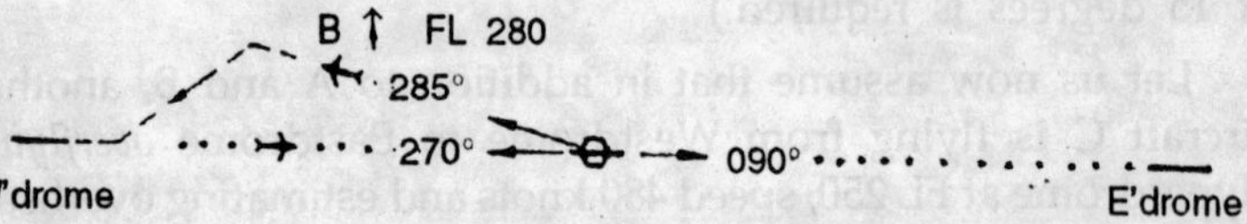

Fig. 3.2 (b)

ATC CLEARANCES (THREE AIRCRAFTS) [3.3 (a) & 3.3 (b)]

TRAFFIC : 'A' arriving Hyperdrome from Westdrome Flight Level 270; Estimated Time of arrival Hyperdrome 1000; Speed 480 knots.

'C' flying from Westdrome to Eastdrome overflying Hyperdrome; Fight Level 250; Estimating overhead Hyperdrome 0955; Speed 480 knots.

'B' departing Hyperdrome for Westdrome; Estimated Time of Departure 0920; Flight Level 280 Speed 480 knots

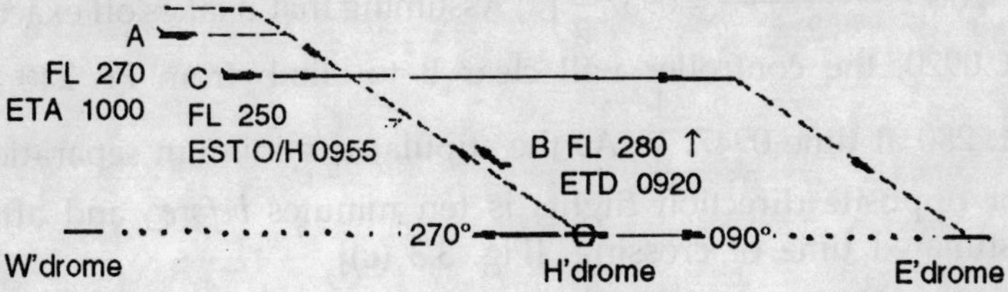

Fig. 3.3 (a)

ClearanceS	:	'C' to continue on 270 radial of Hyperdrome VOR maintaining flight level 250.
		'A' to establish 285 radial of Hyperdrome VOR and then descend from flight level 270.
		'B' to climb on 255 radial of Hyperdrome VOR to flight level 280; Regain track on reaching flight level 280

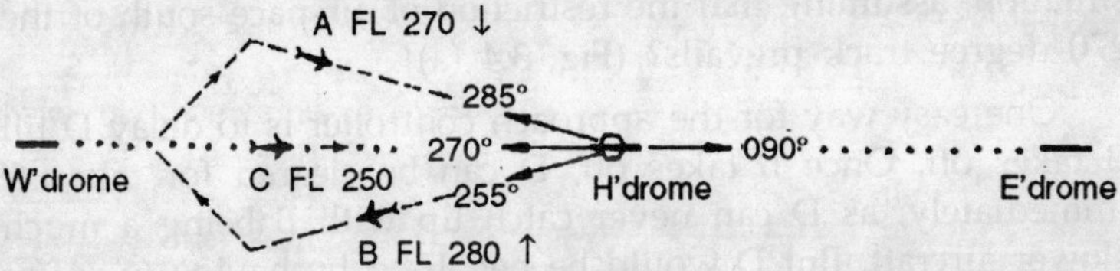

Fig. 3.3 (b)

under restricted conditions to civil flights. (For Delhi FIR, this figure is as high as 70%). So it is not possible to clear B along the 255 radial. How does the approach controller deal with this situation?

It may be noted that in this case with 3 aircraft each one conflicts with the other two. So with 3 aircraft we have three conflicts.

The controller may clear A on 285 radial from Hyperdrome VOR as above. He may clear B on the direct track of 270 degrees to 'climb initially' to FL 240 to maintain separation of 1000 feet from C. Since B and C are same speed aircraft, the approach controller would estimate their 'time of crossing' as $0937\frac{1}{2}$ (Estimated departure time of B is 0920 and estimated time of C overhead Hyperdrome is 0955; crossing time is

$0920 + \frac{0955 - 0920}{2} = 0937\frac{1}{2}\Big)^{*}$. Assuming that B takes off exactly at 0920, the controller will clear B to climb from FL 240 to FL 280 at time 0947 $\frac{1}{2}$. As the stipulated minimum separation for opposite direction flights is ten minutes *before* and after estimated time of crossing. [Fig. 3.3 (c)]

Now complicate the scenario a bit further by assuming that ahead of B another aircraft D is taxiing for take off and bound for Westdrome which has filed a level of 120 and which has a spead of 240 knots, that is half the cruising speed of A, B and C. (Dear reader if you feel that this is becoming too complicated, please skip this; but remember, the controller cannot escape so easily). ATC estimates that D will take off at 0915, that is 5 minutes ahead of B which is also bound for westdrome. How does the approach controller deal with this situation, assuming that the restriction of airspace south of the 270 degree track prevails? (Fig. 3.4 (a)]

One easy way for the approach controller is to delay D till B takes off. Once B takes off, D can be cleared for take off immediately, as D can never catch up with B being a much slower aircraft. But D would be penalised by having to suffer a delay of about 7 minutes (0922-0915, assuming that D takes off 2 minutes after B). If form some reason B is delayed, that delay will be carried over to D. The approach controller may therefore proceed thus;

Clear C to proceed on radial 270 direct to Hyperdrome at FL 250;

Clear D to proceed on radial 270 direct to Westdrome and climb to FL 120;

Clear A to maintain FL 270 and establish on the 285 radial from Hyperdrome VOR and when so established to descend to FL 140;

Clear B to proceed via the 285 radial from Hyperdrome and climb to FL 130; then maintaining FL 130 to establish on the

* It is assumed for the sake of simplicity that the speed of B while climbing is the same as that while cruising which is not correct.

ATC CLEARANCES (THREE AIRCRAFTS) WITH AIRSPACE RESTRICTION AIRSPACE

CLEARANCES : 'A' to establish 285 radial of Hyperdome VOR and then descend from flight level 270.

'C' to continue on 270 radial of Hyperdrome VOR maintaining flight level 250.

'B' to climb on 270 radial of Hyperdrome VOR to flight level 240; Maintain flight level 240 till (time) 0947 $^{1}/_{2}$; Thereafter climb to flight level 280

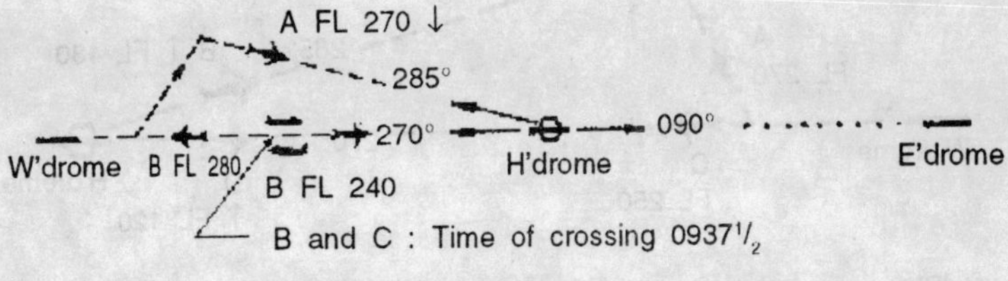

Fig. 3.3 (c)

ATC CLEARANCES (FOUR AIRCRAFTS) (FIG. 3.4 (A) & 3.4 (B))

TRAFFIC : 'A' arriving Hyperdrome from Westdrome; Flight Level 270; Estimated Time of Arrival Hyperdrome 100; Speed 480 knots.

'C' flying from Westdrome to Eastdrome overflying Hyperdrome; Flight Level 250; Estimating overhead Hyperdrome 0955; Speed 480 knots.

'D' departing Hyperdrome for Westdrome; Estimated Time of Departure 0915; Flight Level 120; Speed 240 knots.

'B' departing Hyperdrome for Westdrome; Estimated Time of Departure 0920; Flight Level 280; Speed 480 knots

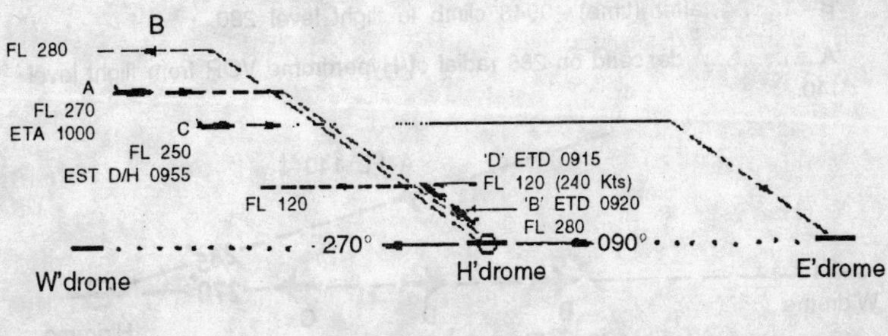

Fig. 3.4 (a)

ATC Clearances (Four aircrafts)

'C' to continue on 270 radial of Hyperdrome VOR maintaining flight level 250

'D' to climb on 270 radial of Hyperdrome VOR to flight level 120

'B' to establish on 285 radial of Hyperdome VOR, then climb to flight level 130.........

'A' to establish on 285 radial of Hyperdrome VOR maintaining flight level 270.

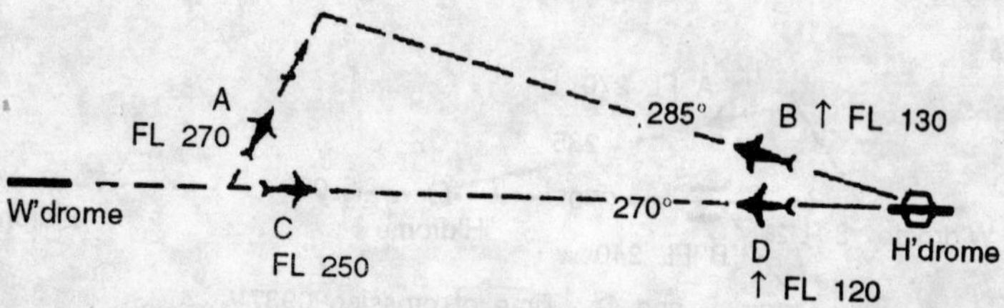

'B' .... maintaining flight level 130 establish 270 radial of Hyperdrome VOR, then climb to flight level 240.............

'A'............descend on 285 radial of Hyperdrome VOR from flight level 270 to flight level 140.............

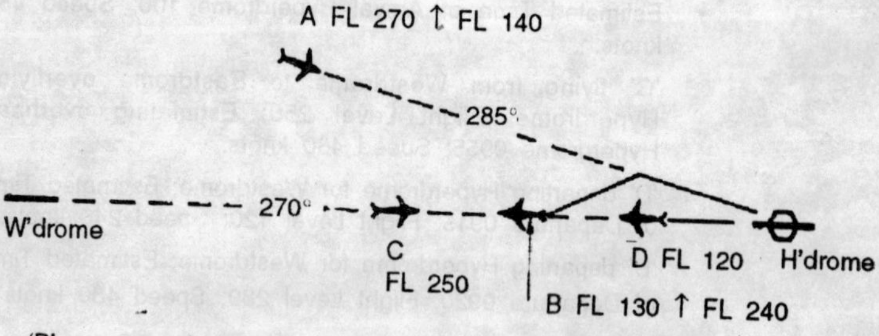

'B' ....after (time) 0948 climb to flight level 280.

'A'............... descend on 285 radial of Hyperdrome VOR from flight level 140.

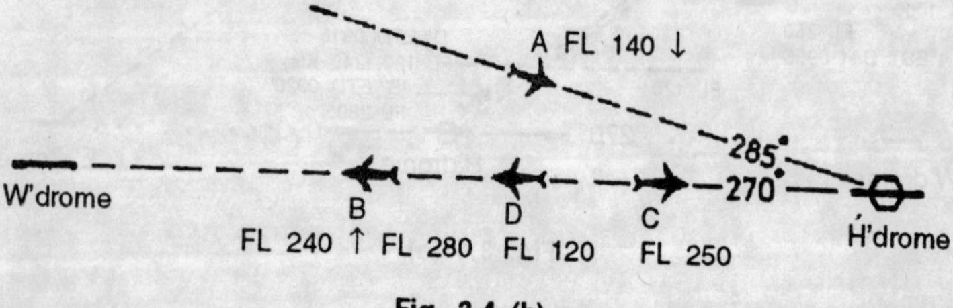

Fig. 3.4 (b)

270 radial from Hyperdrome; When established on the 270 radial to climb to FL 240; Maintain FL 240 till time 0948 and then climb to FL 280.

Clear A to descend below FL 140 *after* B reports established on the 270 radial. (Figure 3.4 (b))

It may be noted that by clearing B on the 285 radial to climb to FL 130, B is separated from D. By restricting B to maintain FL 130 till established on 270 radial and by restricting the level of A to FL 140 (on the 285 radial) B and A are separated. By restricting B to FL 240 till time 0948 B and C are separated as the estimated crossing time is $0937\frac{1}{2}$.

ATC is required to issue prior to take off complete instructions regarding the manoeuvres that should be executed by an aircraft to keep it clear of other traffic, in the process of establishing on its desired track. This is called 'initial air traffic control clearance'. The purpose of issuing this clearance is to guard against the possibility of a communication failure occurring after take off. In the above illustration assuming that the runway at Hyperdrome is North-south runway and D and B take off in a northerly direction the initial air traffic control clearance that will be issued to B and duly 'read back' by him would be as follows;

"B IS CLEARED FROM HYPERDROME TO WESTDROME TO MAINTAIN FLIGHT LEVEL 280. AFTER DEPARTURE, TURN RIGHT TO ESTABLISH RADIAL 285-CLIMB ON RADIAL 285 TO FLIGHT LEVEL 130-TURN LEFT TO ESTABLISH RADIAL 270 MAINTAINING FLIGHT LEVEL 130-CLIMB ON RADIAL 270 TO FLIGHT 240-MAINTAIN TILL TIME 0948 THERAFTER CLIMB TO FLIGHT LEVEL 280".

The above example is not a fanciful one put forward for the purpose of creating an impression, but an example of a situation that could occur in actual practice; and that not once but many times in the course of a single duty of the controller. In fact the illustration is rather a simplified one as it considers traffic in one sector only. Invariably the controller has to deal with traffic from various directions. The situation can become complicated and very involved during periods of peak traffic. It must also be borne in mind that the solutions have to be found as and when the problems arise and cannot be worked out leisurely in advance. This is because the traffic pattern constantly changes and a difference of one or two minutes in the estimates of aircraft drastically alters the scenario. This will give an idea of the mental pressure on the controller and the concentration, mental agility and ingenuity demanded of him.

In the above illustration, it was assumed that at Hyperdrome, VO only was available and that the aerodrome was not equipped with DME (Distance Measuring Equipment). If DME had also been available along with the VO it would have greatly facilitated the handling of the traffic by the controller. The DME provides a continous digital indication of the distance of the aircraft from the aerodrome to the pilot, provided that the aircraft is also fitted with the complementary equipment on board. The DME is a very accurate instrument reliable upto ± 3% of the indicated distance. The precise information on the position of the various aircraft thus available to the ATC through the position reports of the pilot (procedural control, it may be recollected is purely based on reports of position furnished by the pilot) enables the separation to be much reduced. In the absence of DME, the required separation between two aircraft at the same level and on the same track is 15 minutes, which if translated in terms of distance means a separation of 120 nautical miles if the aircraft are maintaining a speed of 480 knots. Whereas with DME, the separation required is only 20 nautical miles. In the case of opposite direction traffic, with DME the separation to be applied is 10 nautical miles after the aircraft have crossed each other. Whereas without DME as already stated, the applicable separation is 10 minutes before or after crossing of the aircraft which means a separation of 80 nautical miles.

The introduction of the DME equipment enabled ATC to handle greater volume of traffic. This is however possible only if all the aircraft concerned are equipped with the complementary equipment. While in the earlier days, this created a problem as all the aircraft were not so fitted, in the present time except for a few vintage aircraft, almost all aircraft carry DME equipment.

The situation described earlier would perhaps been handled in the following manner with the use of DME.

A and C will be cleared direct to Westdrome on the 270 degree radial. A will be cleared to descend to FL 130 utilising the DME to separate it from C; C and A are separated by 5 minutes which is equivalent to 40 NM (nautical miles) much more than the minimum separation of 10 NM required with use of DME. D will also be cleared on the direct track of 270 degree to Westdrome to climb to FL 120. D will cross A at about 100 NM from Hypodrome : A will be cleared to descend below FL 130 after it is established with the help of DME that A and D have crossed each other and are more than 10 NM apart. B would be cleared to climb on the 285 degree radial to FL 260 that is above the level of C at 250 and then asked to establish on the track of 270 from Hypodrome-by that time A would have descended well below FL 260.

This way only B is diverted from its track and A gets its descent in steps. D and C are not disturbed. (Fig. 3.5).

The use of radar in the control of air traffic further facilitated the work of the air traffic controller as very precise information of the positions of the aircraft were independently available to him. This enabled the (horizontal) separation between aircraft to be reduced to as low as 5 miles. Radar control also calls for a similar degree of concentration and mental agility and resourcefulness as procedural control, and in addition a special kind of skill. Radar is provided only within areas where the density of the traffic is very high : Under radar control therefore, the controller is called upon to handle much greater volume of traffic, generally, than under procedural control.

Radar control may be effected to two ways. In the first, known as tactical vectoring, the controller after 'identifying', the aircraft (that is, correlates a particular 'blip' with a particular aircraft) issues to the pilot a series of 'headings' along with appropriate climb or descent instructions. The pilot is required to fly as per the headings given by the controller. An arising aircraft is this 'positioned' by the controller on the final approach of a runway or a departing aircraft, by the issue of appropriate headings is manoeuvred clear of other aircraft until it is established on its intended route. When the traffic is heavy, some aircraft would have to be 'held' in the air while awaiting their turn to land. The controller vectors the aircraft to weave

ATC CLEARANCES (FOUR AIRCRAFT) USING DME

CLEARANCES :

'B' to establish 285 radial of Hyperdrome VOR, then climb to flight level 260............

'C' to continue on 270 radial of Hyperdrome VOR maintaining flight level 250.

'A' to continue on 270 radial of Hyperdrome VOR and descend to flight level 130 using DME to separate it from 'C'..................

'D' to climb on 270 radial of Hyperdrome VOR to flight level 120.

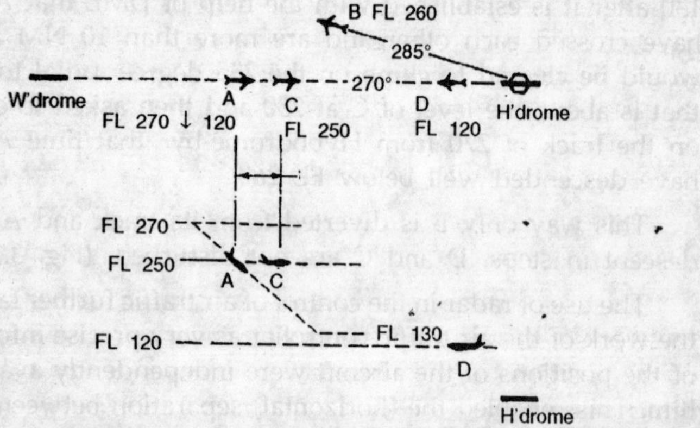

'B' .... to regain track (270 radial of Hyperdrome VOR) climbing to flight level 280.

'A' .... to descend through flight level 120 using DME to separate it from 'D'.

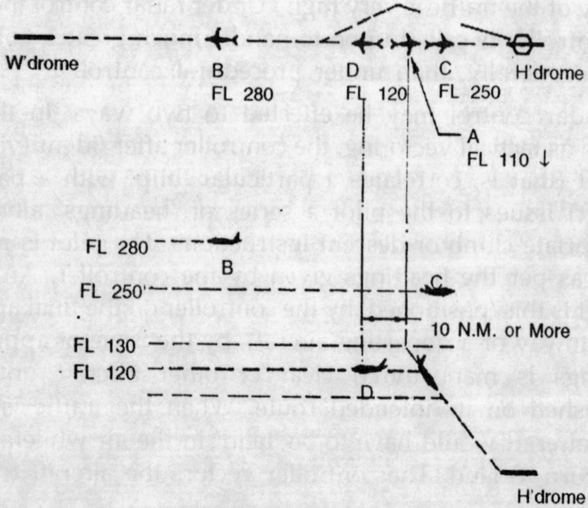

Fig. 3.5

crazy patterns* in the sky until its turn comes and it can be vectored for the final approach.

In the second method of radar control, the routes that the aircraft are to fly are fixed (pre-determined to use a favourite aviation term) and the role of the controller is to keep a watch on the aircraft (that is no active vectoring) and to intervene and to give appropriate instructions to ensure that the minimum separation is not infringed.

In the earlier days the type of radars used for air traffic control purposes were known as primary radars. These radars provided information on the distances and directions of the aircraft from the aerodrome but not their altitudes. The aircraft were represented on the radar screen as arcs. The controller had to keep a sharp watch on the various 'blips' to take care that there was no mix-up in the identifications of the aircraft. In addition he had to keep a mental note of the headings issued to the aircraft (under tactical vectoring) and the levels assigned to the aircraft. The headings issued and the levels assigned keep changing; So much so, if the controller were handing 8 aircrafts at a time, he had to keep track of the identity of these 8 aircrafts and also the current headings and levels of these 8 aircrafts.

An advanced version of the radar, the secondary surveillance radar (SSR) was introduced in the sixties. This radar presents the aircraft in the form of 'synthetic' blips; shape of the blip can be in any desired form. Further, along with the blip relevant information regarding the flight is also tagged; that is information concerning the callsign of the aircraft, speed of the aircraft, level of the aircraft and so on. This information also moves along with the blip. It may be noted that the radar provides information on the altitude also. This relieves the controller of the need to keep watch so as not to lose the identification of the aircraft as also the need to mentally keep note of the levels.

From the above an impression might perhaps been gathered that the progressive introduction of facilities like the DME, primary and then the secondary radar has simplified the work of the controller to the extent that it has become a mechanical

* Sometimes referred to as 'Jilabis' by pilots. !

task devoid of the rough and tumble of the earlier days. This is not correct. While the tools have improved, the challenges have also correspondingly, and in many cases disproportionately increased due to manifold increase of air traffic and progressive reduction of minimum separation.

If procedural control is akin to fighting with a club, radar control is like fighting with a rapier—the weapon is more refined but the challenges are also a match for the weapon.

The impression might also perhaps been gathered that procedural control is totally extinct. This is far from true. Radars and associated equipment are expensive and are provided only at aerodromes where the volume of traffic warrants such expenditure. As stated earlier, at a majority of aerodromes both within India and abroad procedural control is in vogue.

At this stage it may be interesting and enlightening to see how airspace capacity is related to the criteria of minimum standard separation applied, which in turn depends on the type of facilities available. If we assume that all aircraft are maintaining a true airspeed of 480 knots then the spacing between successive aircraft flying on the same track and at the same level will be equal to

— A; 120 nautical miles if procedural separation (longitudinal separation based on time) is applied.

— B; 80 nautical miles if procedural separation (longitudinal separation based on time) is applied in areas where navigation aids permit frequent determination of position and speed.

— C; 20 nautical miles if procedural separation (longitudinal separation based on distance) is applied using DME.

— D; 5 nautical miles if radar separation is applied.

— E; 3 nautical miles if reduced radar separation minimum is applied.

It will be seen that application of longitudinal separation

based on distance using DME (C) increases airspace capacity six times, application of radar separation of 5 miles (D) increases airspace capacity by 24 times and application of radar separation of 3 miles (E) increases airspace capacity by 40 times relative to the airspace capacity obtained when longitudinal separation based on time (A) is applied.

We can similarly illustrate how use of the radar can drastically reduce delays for landing aircraft. Assume that six aircraft are approaching an aerodrome from different directions with the same ETAs (estimated times of arrival). The aerodrome had one instrument-approach-to-land procedure which takes five minutes from the time of leaving the holding pattern. There is no radar at the aerodrome. The meteorological conditions are such that all the aircraft have to carry out the full instrument approach to land procedure.

It is easy to see that the cumulative delay will be equal to 0 + 5 + 10 + 15 + 20 + 25 = 75 minutes.

Now assume that a radar facility is available at the aerodrome. If a horizontal separation of 5 nautical miles is applied using radar, the time interval between successive landings will be approximately two minutes (taking average approach speed as 150 knots). The cumulative delay will therefore be equal to 0 + 2 + 4 + 6 + 8 + 10 = 30 minutes.

In other words there is a saving of 45 minutes. Such savings of time means not merely less expenditure on fuel but savings of valuable time of the passengers. One can verily say therefore that a radar is worth its weight in gold !

We had so far been on the subject of approach control service, that is separation of aircraft arriving at and departing from an aerodrome. The next aspect of the controllers' job is the separation of traffic when they are nicely settled on their tracks and are in what is known as the en-route phase of the flight. The aircraft have reached their desired flight levels and are now cruising steadily within a network of routes as they head for their respective destinations. The controller has to keep a surveillance on these flights to ensure that there is no danger of collision.

Possibilities of collisions in the en-route phase may arise due to various circumstances; due to two or more routes crossing each other or due to a following aircraft being faster than a preceding one at the same level; or as a result of new aircraft, that is aircraft that have just departed from an aerodrome joining the air route. Potential collisions could also arise in the process of aircraft changing their levels en-route. For reasons of fuel conservation, aircraft tend to climb to higher levels as they progressively become lighter on account of consumption of their own fuel, as the rate of fuel consumption at higher levels is less. While so clearing them, the controller has to guard against the possibility of collision with another aircraft on the same track (through the level of which the subject aircraft may be climbing) or with another aircraft flying in the opposite direction or with another aircraft on an entirely different route, but converging with or crossing the route of the subject aircraft at some distance point.

Even if the aircraft are not changing levels and everything appears to be going smoothly and their seems to be no possibility of collision, the controller has to keep a watch to satisfy himself that the flights are operating normally. Under procedural control this is achieved by means of periodic position reports from the aircraft. Non receipt of an expected position report would alert the controller to the possibility that all is not well with the flight. Under radar control, the controller himself has the aircraft in view, as it were, all the time.

I have briefly explained how the controller fulfils his basic task of preventing collisions between aircraft while at the same time endeavouring to expedite and maintain an orderly flow of air traffic by the issue of appropriate clearances. These tasks comprise items (1), (2) and (3) of the Objectives of Air Traffic Services (page 11). There are two other objectives *i.e.* items (4) and (5) which through not directly related to the active control of air traffic are nevertheless very important.

Item (4) of the Objectives of Air Traffic Services is to 'Provide advice and information useful for the safe and efficient conduct of flights'. The transmissions from the air traffic controller to the pilot invariably comprise messages either in the category of 'clearances' or 'information' (apart, of course from courtesies like 'thank you', 'good morning', 'have a nice day'!). The information provided to the pilot may be of various kinds. It may be just a 'time check'—air traffic control units are expected to provide time information correct upto half-a-minute. It may comprise meteorological data, aerodrome data like runway-in-use and so on. It may also relate to information on aerodrome condition like water on the runway, construction work in progress or activity of firing ranges which information, it is felt, the pilot may have no knowledge of though, already dirseminated to all concerned aerodromes, on account of the time factor.

Item (5) of the Objective of Air Traffic Services is to 'Notify appropriate organisations regarding aircraft in need of search and rescue aid and assist such organisations as required'. The controller is the vital link between the pilot in the air and rest of the world on the ground. In the event of an emergency, it is the controller on whom the pilot depends for assistance; the controller may render assistance himself or coordinate with and mobilise other agencies who can render the required assistance.

In the training of controllers, emergency handling is given considerable importance. Controllers are rigorously trained to deal with various kinds of aircraft emergencies. At the Civil Aviation Training Centre, Allahabad in the initial training of controllers, the exercises are set for handling of two simultaneous emergency situations. Probability of two emergencies occuring simultaneously is extremely small; more than two is as unlikely as lightning striking thrice in the same place !

ICAO DOC 4444 lays down procedures for handling of some types of emergencies by the controller; while doing so, it also recognises that the various circumstances surrounding each emergency situation precludes the establishment of detailed procedures to be followed and that air traffic control units should use their best judgement in handling the emergency situations; it is therefore clear that emergency situations put the controller's mettle on real test.

DOC 4444 provides guidance on dealing with the following 'in-flight contingencies'.

—AIR GROUND COMMUNICATION FAILURE : DOC 4444 details the procedures to be followed and action to be taken by the pilot as well as the controller when an aircraft experiences air ground communications failure. Thus, the pilot completely cut off from the world need not panic, but has just to comply with the procedures, fully secure in the knowledge that the air traffic control would be fully aware of what he is doing and would take appropriate measures.

—UNLAWFUL INTERFERENCE : Popularly known as 'hijacking'. In the wake of a new development in the form of seizing control of an aircraft by threatening to blow it up with explosives adopted by some individuals and terrorist organisations beginning from the early seventies, the ICAO developed some basic procedures in 1974 for air traffic control to respond to such situations. The emphasis on these procedures is on the need for the air traffic control to recognize that an aircraft is under unlawful interference, the need to provide all possible assistance to the aircraft in its flight and the need to anticipate the requirements of the aircraft for information relating to air navigation in view of the fact that it is likely to deviate from its current flight plan. For today's air passengers who have accepted the stringent requirements of security in the form of being subjected to a security check, having to be virtually held prisoner in the departure holding area and so in it may sound inconceivable that there was a time when passengers used to merrily check in and wait in the lounge and nonchalantly board the aircraft on announcement of the departure.

—STRAYED OR UNIDENTIFIED AIRCRAFT : A Korean Airlines Boeing 747 carrying 269 passengers plus crew was on flight from New York to Seoul on 1st September 1983. It apparently strayed into Soviet airspace near the highly sensitive Sakhalin Island military installation to the north of Japan. The aircraft was shot down by a Soviet fighter. It was hit by an air-to-air missile at 35,000 feet. The crippled airliner dropped to 19,000 feet in just four minutes and it was another terrifying eight minutes before is smashed into the sea. There were no survivors.

The shooting down of the Korean Airliner created world wide concern. The ICAO incorporated procedures in the DOC 4444 in 1986 for handling of strayed and unidentified aircraft to safeguard against shooting down of civil aircraft that may have strayed from their intended tracks.

The above are all 'inflight contingencies'. In the event of an actual actual aircraft accident, the controller plays the key role of mobilising the forces and agencies that can physically provide succour to the unfortunate aircraft and its occupants. Air traffic control units are provided with emergency plans and the controllers are trained to be fully familiar and act in accordance with such plans.

There are two types of emergency plans. The first is in respect of aircraft accidents on or in the vicinity of aerodromes and is called "Airport Emergency Plan'. Airports are generally equipped with rescue and fire fighting services, the scale of the equipment depending upon the types of aircraft using that airport and the number of movements at that airport. The emergency plan details the action to be taken by the controller and each of the agencies that have a role to play in the succour of the crashed aircraft.

The second type of plan is in respect of aircraft accidents away from the airports. It is called the Search and Rescue plan. The aircraft may have crashed in remote areas and a search may have to be mounted to locate that aircraft before undertaking rescue effort. This action is coordinated by the Rescue Coordination Centre (RCC). The search and rescue plan sets our details of the various agencies like the air force, army, navy, coast guard, police and so on who can assist in the search and rescue effort. In India aerial search is generally undertaken by the Air Force or the Navy aircraft. The air traffic control plays a vital part in the efficiency coordination of the search and rescue effort.

In aircraft accidents, time is of the utmost essence in the saving of the lives of the victims. Studies show that while the initial survivors of an aircraft crash have less than 10% chance of survival if rescue is delayed beyond two days, the survival rate is over 60% if rescue can be accomplished within 8 hours. When an aircraft crashes in remote areas it may take from a few house to a few months for the wreckage to be located, when a physical search is conducted. (Most readers will be aware that the Air India B 707 which crashed over Mount Blanc in Central Europe in the sixties defied all attempts to locate the wreckage until, after many years it was found due to the dedicated search carried out by the son of one of the victims.)

A system was developed in the late eighties to detect and locate a crashed aircraft immediately after the occurrence of the accident. This system called the 'COSPAS SARSAT' system is based on satellite technology. It works on the following principle.

There are six dedicated satellites orbiting the earth in appoximately polar orbits, three of them launched by the C.I.S. and three by the U.S.A. The emergency locater transmitter (ELT) carried on board the aircraft, gets activated automatically in the event of an accident, due to the force of the impact. The beacons emit signals on frequencies 121.5 MHz. or 406 MHz depending on its type. These signals are picked up by one or more of the orbitting satellites which may be in view of the location of the crashed aircraft. The signals are retransmitted by the satellites and picked up by a ground station (technically called Local User Terminal) which computes the location of the crashed aircraft in terms of geographical coordinates (Fig. 3.6) and automatically sends an 'alert' to the concerned rescue coordination centre (RCC).

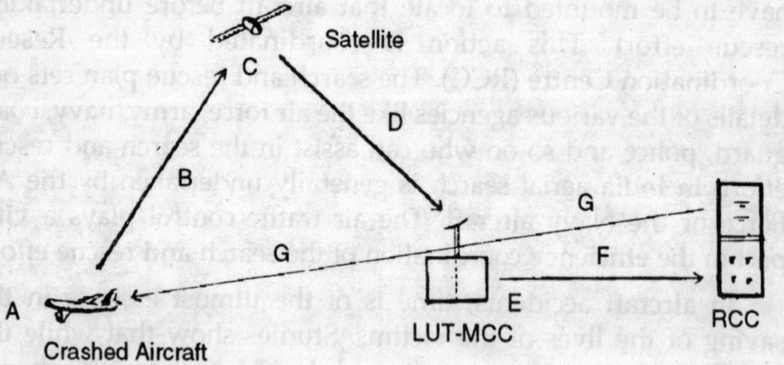

Fig. 3.6 : Sarsat System

A. Aircraft crashes in remote area;

B. ELT (Emergency Locater Transmitter) gets activated and emits signals;

C. Search & Rescue Satellite picks up the signals;

D. Search & Rescue satellite retransmits the signals;

E. Lut-MCC (Local User Terminal—Mission Control Centre) picks up the signals and calculates the position of the crashed aircraft;

F. LUT-MCC sends an alert signal to RCC (Rescue Coordination Centre);

G. RCC activates Search & Rescue;

India is a participant of the COSPAS SARSAT System. The Indian Space Research Organisation (ISRO) has established a Local User Terminal (LUT) and Mission Control Centre (MCC) at Bangalore in 1990. Rescue Coordination Centre (RCC) Bombay was the first RCC to be linked to this LUT-MCC. Later another LUT-MCC was established at Lucknow. Now all the 4 RCCS in India are linked to the SARSAT System.

The system has been working in India for nearly 7 years now. In actual practice it suffers from one serious drawback which considerably limits its usefulness. This is on account of the fact that numerous 'false alerts' are received. These false alerts by 'crying wolf' too often tend to make the controller treat them casually as it is just impossible to react to every one of them. It is therefore easily possible to overlook one genuine alert in the face of an overwhelmingly large number of false ones. It is learnt that the number of false alerts have progressively reduced. Perhaps technological improvements in the future may enable total elimination of such false alerts so that the system becomes truly dependable.

4

Thrills and Throes of Air Traffic Control

My long career as an air traffic controller commenced on the 18th of June in the year 1959 at Chennai International Airport and terminated after a span of about 36 years at the Headquarters of the Airports Authority of India at New Delhi. During this period I had worked at a number of aerodromes in India. The important airports at which I had worked were; Chennai Airport for a total period of about 14 years in two terms from 1959 to 1964 and then again from 1978 to 1987; Calcutta Airport from 1969 to 1976 and Mumbai Airport from 1987 to 1992. Chennai and Mumbai Airports were of course known as Madras and Bombay Airports in those days.

I was only nominally an air traffic controller when I took over as assistant aerodrome officer at Madras Airport during June 1959 after completion of my training at the Civil Aviation Training Centre, Allahabad. Further training has to be undergone at the Chennai Airport before I was declared qualified to perform actual duties. The training comprised 'on-the-job' training for a minimum prescribed period under an experienced controller followed by a written test in which knowledge of the procedures applicable at Chennai Airport was assessed and followed by a practical examination in which a board of experienced controllers observed actual handling of the traffic; and finally a viva voce by a board of experienced controllers. If the performance was assessed as meeting the required standard then a 'rating' was conferred which entitled one to work independently at that unit. The same procedure of 'rating' was applicable to every other ATC unit.

A controller, even if he holds all the ratings at one airport, on transfer to some other airport, has to acquire the ratings in respect of all the units at that airport by the same process. This is somewhat of a humiliating experience as the controller may have to carry out on-the-job training under other controllers who may well be his juniors in service. When I was transferred to Mumbai Airport from Chennai Airport in 1987, I was holding the rank of deputy director and was also the designated instructor for Madras Airport. Still I had to acquire all the ratings at Bombay Airport and in the process perform on-the-job training duties under controllers who very holding the rank of Aerodrome Officers. However, humiliating this may be there is no other way. This stringent process of training and acquiring ratings is essential in view of the tremendous responsibility for the safety of human lives that is placed in the hands of the controller. When he is allowed to sit in the controller's chair all by himself, it requires to be ensured beyond doubt, that he is physically, mentally, emotionally and professionally fit to undertake the responsibility entrusted to him.

However, in most other countries the controller is not required to acquire ratings for all the units. He specializes in one or at the most two units and continues to perform duties in that or those two units. He is also not normally shifted from one aerodrome to another like his Indian counterpart. This way, a lot of stress on the controller incidental to having to go through the process of frequently acquiring ratings is avoided; as well as loss of time involved in such frequent training for the controllers.

In the course of my long career, I had put in a great number of hours in air traffic control duties, working round the clock in different environments and in a variety of situations. As a purely procedural controller at Chennai in the early stages of my career; as a procedural and radar controller at Calcutta during the years when traffic was very high at Calcutta (upto the year 1960, of all airports in India, Calcutta had the maximum traffic. Step by step it was overtaken by Mumbai and then by

Delhi); again as procedural and radar controller at Chennai; then as a radar and procedural controller at Mumbai which at that time boasted (and still boasts) the heaviest traffic of all airports in India. I had experienced many a thrilling moment. I had gone through many anxious and nerve racking situations. I had undergone many a moment of intense mental pressure and I have also been rewarded with sheer sense of accomplishment and fulfilment. Some of those experiences that still linger on my sub-conscious are narrated in the following pages.

The earlier recollection is regarding an incident involving an air force aircraft crash during my first year of working as an air traffic controller at Chennai. The crash involved an air force trainer aircraft which had taken off from Tambaram, an Indian Air Force Airfield situated very close to Chennai Airport. Tambaram was a training school for flying instructors. IAF aircraft, in those days mostly Harvards, used to take off from Tambaram and proceed to their local flying area, south of Chennai. While flying in that area they kept in contact with Madras Approach; calling up Madras Approach when leaving Tambaram, then while flying in the local flying area, reporting 'operations normal' every 15 minutes, and then calling up Madras Approach once again after completion of their flying to inform that they are returning to Tambaram. That day one such aircraft whose callsign was 'One Zero Two' has taken off at about 7:45 in the morning. The pilot, as I learnt later was Fit. Lt. R. 28 years of age, an accomplished flier and instructor. That was the last sortie he was to fly as he was due to proceed on leave from the next day for his wedding.

'102' called up Madras Approach and reported duration of flying as 30 minutes. I instructed him as per the routine procedure to 'Report operations normal every 15 minutes. The aircraft acknowledged the message. At about 8:05, since '102' had not called, I gave a couple of calls to him. There was no response and I repeated the calls at intervals of a minute. I did not think that there was a cause for alarm as quite frequently, the training aircraft get so absorbed in their exercises that they forgot to give routine 'Ops normal' calls.

At about 8:10 I received a call from '102' to inform me that he was returning to Tambaram. I acknowledged and 'deleted'

'102' from my board, marking the time of the call. To my surprise and consternation, at about 8:20 or so, Tambaram told me on telephone that '102' had not yet landed back and asked me whether I was in contact with the aircraft. I told ATC Tambaram that '102' has called me up at 8:10 to inform that he was returning to Tambaram and that I had no further contact or message.

But as it transpired, '102' had neither contacted ATC Tambaram nor landed there. There was no response to further calls from ATC Tambaram or Madras approach. It was becoming evident that the aircraft had suffered a mishap. Then at about 9:00 information was received from some villagers about an aircraft that had crashed at a place south of Madras. The pilot, as per their information, had not survived the crash.

An inquiry was instituted by the Air Force authorities. But before the inquiry was held I came to know that the pilot's watch damaged in the crash had stopped working and was indicating time 8:00 exactly.

It was quite clear from the above that the Aircraft must have crashed at 8:00. This was highly disconcerting and puzzling to me. I had noted the time of the last call as 8:10 and in my statement too I had mentioned that the aircraft had last contacted me at that time. There was no possibility of my mistaking the time of the call as I had made a series of entries on my board before and after the call and the chronological order to the entries tallied.

The inquiry was carried out by the Air Force authorities. All the relevant documents including the tapes had been sealed as per the usual procedure. It may be mentioned that every exchange of message on every frequency between the pilots and air traffic control as well as all telephone conversations emanating and terminating at all air traffic control units are continuously recorded. On the occurrence of a crash or any incident calling for an inquiry these tapes are immediately sealed and kept in safe custody so as to guard against the possibility of tampering.

I sought and was given permission to be present during the time the tapes were played back. Needless to say, I was worried and puzzled. When the tapes were replayed it went something like this;

Time	From	To	Message
07 : 45	102	Madras App	Madras—One Zero Two
07 : 45	Madras App	102	One Zero Two Go Ahead
07: 45	102	Madras App	Proceeding to Local Flying Area—Duration Thirty Minutes
07 : 45	Madras App	102	One Zero Two Roger-Report Operations Normal Every One Five Minutes
08 : 05	Madras App	102	One Zero Two Madras—Do You Read (repeated a number of times)
08 : 10	Volga 22	Madrass App	Madras Volga Two Two
08 : 10	Madras App	Volga 22	One Zero Two-Go Ahead
08 : 10	Volga 22	Madras App	Volga Two Two Returning to Tambaram
08 : 10	Madras App	Volga 22	One Zero Two Roger—Over to Tambaram

So the mystery was solved. It was confusion of call signs between Volga 22 and '102' caused by phonetic similarity in the callsigns, Volga 22 had not contacted me when proceeding to the local flying area; perhaps, he tried to call but the frequency was busy. So the error had occurred due to coincidence-Volga 22 failing to contact me initially and similarity in the callsign.

The investigation report apparently did not lay any blame on me as I was not questioned further. I breathed a deep sigh of relief.

However, on recapitulating the incident a few years later. I felt that I should not have made the mistake that I had done. I had misheard Volga 22 for '102' *because '102' was what I was expecting to hear.* This is one of the pitfalls of air traffic control; that the controller expects a certain routine response and if it happens to be different his mind may not register it. The controller has to guard against this and requires to be alert all the time. After some experience he does't give in to such errors. In my own case, if the incident had occurred a couple of years later, I feel that I would not have made the mistake.

In the above case, the error was not of much significance. There have been instances where similar errors have resulted in potentially dangerous situations. I have known at least 3 cases where controllers had erred in properly noting the flight levels of aircraft due to the actual level maintained by the aircraft being different from the expected level. One such case concerned an Scandinavian Airways DC8 which was flying from some airport in Europe to Singapore at FL 370; ATC Mumbai had earlier received the FL as 330. The aircraft had subsequently climbed to FL 370 somewhere while flying in the Middle East, but for some reason ATC Mumbai had not received the 'change' message. The aircraft flew through the entire Mumbai airspace, reporting 'FL 370' at 4 reporting points and the controller routinely reading back as 'FL 330'; curiously the pilot also failed to notice and correct the wrong read back. The error came to light when the Scandinavian Airways DC8 had a near collision with an Indian Airlines aircraft, while entering Chennai airspace. The Chennai controller had assumed the level of the Scandinavian DC 8 to be FL 330 on the basis of information received from Mumbai ATC and he had allotted FL 370 to the Indian Airlines aircraft. This incident took place in 1992.

A controller has to listen to the transmissions of the aircraft with utmost concentration. If he fails to pick up any message from an aircraft and this may happen at times on account of the poor quality of the equipment or due to differences in accents, he cannot just afford to dismiss the transmission as unimportant. He has to ask the aircraft to 'Say again'. I remember an incident which also occurred at Chennai during my early years. A British Airways aircraft had landed in the night at about 10:00 P.M. After landing and while approaching his parking stand on the apron he called up the tower and informed that 'While landing some animals crossed our path; we don't know whether we hit them'. The controller who was new could not pick up this message which has delivered very fast and in a typical British accent.

Since the aircraft had already landed and was about to switch off on the parking stand he thought that the message was nothing important and so he merely said 'Roger'. He thereafter allowed another aircraft, an Indian Airlines Viscount, which was holding, to take off from the same runway. The pilot of this aircraft noticed a dead cow right in the middle of the runway during the take off run, and he pulled up sharply and avoided the dead animal. He immediately informed the tower.

The matter was taken very seriously and an inquiry was instituted.

The tape recording was replayed and I was also present during the replay. This particular transmission regarding the animals on the runway was delivered so fast and in such a typical British accent that it had to be replayed again and again before we could make out what the pilot was saying. No wonder, the controller missed it. However, he did not ask the pilot to repeat the message in which case he would have understood the message.

The inquiry did not blame the controller for allowing the British Airways aircraft to land when there were animals on the runway. The controller had taken all action as required by the rules to check the runway prior to the landing of the aircraft. There were many gaps in the aerodrome fencing—the inquiry committee counted as many as 64 gaps—and under such circumstances it was held that the controller could not be blamed. But the Committee held that the controller had erred in allowing the Indian Airlines Viscount to take off after having been informed of the presence of animals on the runway.

One of the controllers' cardinal responsibilities is to ensure that the runway is free of obstacles when aircraft are landing or taking off. This responsibility devolves on him by virtue of item (2) of the Objectives of Air Traffic Services; "To prevent collisions between aircraft on the manoeuvring area and obstructions on that area". Manoeuvring area includes runways and taxiways and obstructions for this purpose means vechicular traffic or other non-permanent obstructions. The pilot is entirely dependant on the controller for ensuring that his take off or landing is safe in this respect. Every time that the controller clears an aircraft to land, he makes sure that the runway is actually clear of all obstructions like personnel, cattle or vechicles. During the day he checks the runway visually that is by 'running his eyes' over the entire length of the runway and during periods of darkness or in bad visibility, he has the runway 'Checked by a jeep.'

Since aerodromes are generally for away from the cities and surrounded by villages, intrusion of cattle etc into the aerodrome and on the runway is quite common. In the earlier days this problem was existing at all aerodromes, big and small as the aerodromes were protected only by a barbed wire fencing. However, a bold decision was made by somebody to solve this problem permanently at least in the case of the larger airports. That is, to build a wall all around the aerodrome. I call this a 'bold' decision because the financial implications must have been frightening. The perimeter of an aerodrome is as long as 6-10 km and a wall of this length is terribly expensive to build. However such walls were built one by one around the bigger airports and the cattle problem vanished. Still, even today, at most of the aerodromes only barbed wire fencing is available and controllers have to be wary of intrusion of cattle on to the runway.

In the states of U.P. and Bihar bluebulls pose a source of hazard to aircraft. These bluebulls (nilgays) which roam about freely, are greyish of colour and have the appearance, partly of a horse and partly of a mule. They are not slaughtered for the table by the people of these states, who, I am told, hold these animals in veneration. The bluebulls stray on to the airfields and have on many occasions been hit by aircraft landing or taking off. Lucknow, Varanasi and Patna aerodromes are particularly susceptible to the problem of bluebull intrusion. As late as in 1992, there was an instance of an aircraft hitting a bluebull at Lucknow. Since killing of these animals is not permitted, approval had to be obtained from the District Magistrate for shooting a few of them for the safety of the aircraft.

Apart from cattle or bluebulls there have been fairly recent incidents of an Air India B 747 hitting a jeep while landing at Bombay in 1994; and an Indian Airlines A 300 hitting a cyclist while landing at Hyderabad in 1995. The controller has therefore to be very careful while clearing aircraft for landing or for take off, to prevent the possibility of an accident.

Talking of accidents, a controller gets worried and spends sleepless nights if there happens to be an accident during his tour of duty, even under circumstances where it may appear that ATC could not be even remotely responsible for the crash.

This is because in almost every aircraft accident or incident the role of ATC is minutely investigated. There is an attempt to ascribe some fault of commission or omission to the controller. The investigating authority as well as the airline company's lawyers pore through all the documents, circulars, instruction etc. concerning ATC and subject the controller to an intense interrogation as to his understanding of the rules and regulations, knowledge of procedures as also his handling of the traffic during the accident or incident. The lawyers try to trap and confuse the controller into inconsistencies. Generally speaking, controllers, except for a very few do not possess the legal temperment or turn of mind. Their is a job where you have no time to split hairs or leisurely analyse a situation. You have to get the job done even, if it means cutting corners at times. Moreover, the various rules and regulations concerning air traffic control, while very comprehensive, never-the-less lend themselves to different interpretations. One has to piece together the various provisions found in different documents and while no doubt they are generally consistent, the full picture is not a clear one.

It is as if they are pieces of a zig-zag puzzle that can be put together to give various somewhat different but coherent pictures. During the process of investigation by courts of inquiries, there have been instances when a single provision of the ICAO DOC 4444 has been debated and mercilessly analysed for hours with the controller standing in the witness box all the time. I have known controllers who subjected to this ordeal had literally aged ten years by the time the investigation was completed.

Speaking of myself, apart from the accident to the Indian Air Force Trainer mentioned earlier one other accident occurred in the course of my career during the period I was on duty. It happened long ago at Agartala aerodrome where I had been sent on temporary duty from Calcutta airport in 1969. Agartala aerodrome is very close to Bangladesh—which was still East Pakistan at that time-and in fact the aerodrome fencing was and still is, the international boundary. During the Indo-Pak War of 1965 one trigger happy Pakistani fighter pilot had flown past the old control tower of Agartala aerodrome spraying bullets indiscriminately, killing one control assistant and seriously wounding one air traffic controller who happened to be on duty at that time. After that the old tower was fully walled up with only slits for the controller to look outside.

The accident involved an Indian Airlines Friendship aircraft which was to take off from Guwahati aerodrome, land at Agartala and then take off again for Calcutta. Due to bad weather as it was monsoon time, the pilot had been putting off his departure form Guwahati and finally decided to take off. The weather was bad over Agartala, when the aircraft arrived overhead and dusk was falling. The pilot made couple of abortive attempts to make a landing. In the third attempt, he misjudged the beginning of the runway and touched down well past the normal touchdown zone. On account of the short length of the runway—about 5000 feet as I recollect, and due to the presence of water on the runway (which reduces the braking effect) he could not bring the aircraft to a halt within the remaining length of the runway. As I watched with my heart in my mouth from the tower the aircraft made a deep swerve and then disappeared from view. I immediately called the aircraft on the radio frequency but there was no response. I rushed in the jeep towards the runway end. The aircraft had overshot the runway and settled into a huge ditch which was running across the runway at a distance of about 400 feet from the runway end. Fuel was pouring out but miraculously the aircraft did not catch fire. (If the aircraft had not been 'stopped' by the ditch it would in all probability gone into East Pakistan Territory). I could hear the wailing and shouting of the passengers. I remember to have shouted 'Help is coming'. Immediately after, our crash tender and ambulance reached the spot and assisted the passengers to get out and clear off the area immediately. Luckily there were no casualties—a couple of passengers sustained minor injuries.

Inquiry followed. Since there were no loss of lives (the aircraft was however damaged) the inquiry was only a Departmental one conducted by an officer of the Aeronautical Inspection Wing of the Civil Aviation Department.

The investigation attributed the accident to 'aqua planning' that is presence of water on the runway which forms a thin film between the wheels of the aircraft and the surface of the runway reducing the braking effect.

In the majority of air accidents, ATC is only indirectly involved. In a mid-air collision of course as in the one which took place near Delhi during November 1996, the focus is on ATC as prevention of collisions is the prime responsibility or air traffic control. But apart from this accident, there were two other major accidents in the past in India in which it appeared that there was some severe failure on the part of air traffic control and its role came in for severe scrutiny during the investigation by the Courts of Inquiry.

The first of the two accidents happened just a few months before I joined the Department. It happened at Calcutta airport. A Skyways Hermes aircraft landed in the early morning or rather alighted on the top of another aircraft, a Dakota belonging to a private operator which had lined up for take off on runway 01 L* (L stands for 'left') at Calcutta airport. The Dakota was a freighter bound for Agartala and had only three persons—the crew—on board, that is, the pilot, co-pilot and radio officer, all of them named Choudhary. All the three lost their lives in the accident. The Hermes aircraft somehow managed to effect a safe landing with minor damage to the aircraft and no loss of lives of severe injuries to its passengers.

* Runways are designated by a two digit number between 01 and 36. This two digit number represents in tens of degrees the magnetic heading of the axis of the aircraft when it is aligned on the runway for take off. For example, if a runway is aligned exactly in the East-West (magnetic) direction an aircraft taking off from West to East or an aircraft approaching to land from West to East would be taking off or landing on runway 09 as the aircraft would be heading 090 M while taking off or while landing. If there are parallel runways an additional letter is added to the two digits designating that runway. eg 01 L (01 Left), 01 R (01 Right), 01 C (01 Centre) and so on.

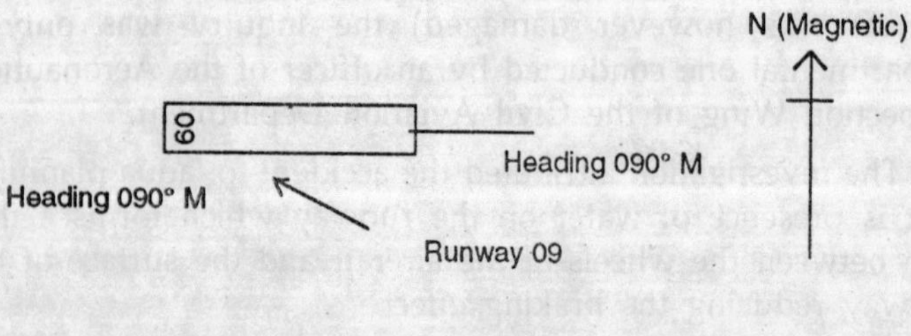

The circumstances were as follows. There were and still are—two parallel North-South runways at Calcutta Airport, separated by a distance of 700 feet which was the minimum spacing required as per ICAO standards at that time (Fig. 4.1). One Position Indicator (PPI) radar had recently been installed at Calcutta. This was a facility by which aircraft could be 'talked down' by the radar controller. That is, the controller with the help of the radar could issue instructions to the aircraft so as to position it in line with the runway at an appropriate height to enable the pilot to sight the runway and make a landing. The Hermes aircraft was given a radar approach for a landing from South to North on runway 01 R (Right) that is the runway which would be on the right as seen by the pilot coming in for landing. The Dakota had positioned itself for take off on runway 01 L. The Hermes aircraft informed the radar controller that the runway was in sight and was accordingly cleared to land on runway 01 R. As it happened the pilot had mistaken left hand runway for the right hand one *i.e.* mistaken 01 L for 01 R. In the process, he alighted on the top of the Dakota with the unfortunate consequences already mentioned.

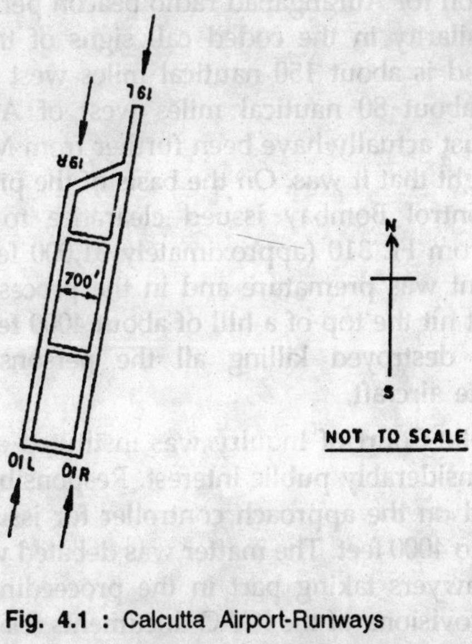

Fig. 4.1 : Calcutta Airport-Runways

ATC was very much in the picture as the aircraft was given a radar approach. The pilot of the Hermes aircraft, a very forthright person, told the Court of Inquiry that he did see something 'shining' at the runway beginning but took it to be water on the runway. The Court of Inquiry exonerated ATC as the responsibility of ATC in a radar approach terminates at a specified altitude (Obstacle Clearance Limit) and beyond and below that point the pilot is fully responsible for subsequent disposition of the aircraft.

In the second of the air accidents referred to, a basic issue regarding the role of ATC in the avoidance of collisions with terrain was examined at considerable length. The accident was in respect of an Alitalia airlines DC 8 and took place in 1963. The aircraft was approaching from the East to land at Mumbai Airport at about midnight and in the process of descending, it struck a hill top to the West/North-West of Mumbai. All the occupants aboard the aircraft were killed.

During the investigations that followed, it was revealed that the pilot of the aircraft had apparently erred in determining the position of the aircraft. He appeared to have mistaken Akola radio beacon for Aurangabad radio beacon perhaps on account of the similarity in the coded call signs of the two beacons. Aurangabad is about 150 nautical miles west of Mumbai and Akola is about 80 nautical miles west of Aurangabad. The aircraft must actually have been further from Mumbai than the pilot thought that it was. On the basis of the pilot's report, Air Traffic Control Bombay issued clearance to the aircraft to descend from FL 310 (approximately 31,000 feet) to 4000 feet. The descent was premature and in the process of descending the aircraft hit the top of a hill of about 4000 feet in height and was fully destroyed killing all the persons on board the unfortunate aircraft.

A public Court of Inquiry was instituted and the inquiry evoked considerably public interest. Responsibility was sought to be fixed on the approach controller for issuing the descent clearance to 4000 feet. The matter was debated with learned and eminent lawyers taking part in the proceedings of the court. Various provisions of the ICAO documents relating to air traffic control were analysed threadbare.

The objectives of air traffic services as laid down by ICAO in Annex 11-Air Traffic Services, do not specify prevention of collisions with terrain as one of the objectives. Further DOC 4444—Rules of the Air and Air Traffic Services states by way of a 'Note; "The objectives of air traffic control services as prescribed in Annex 11 do not include prevention of collision with terrain. The procedures prescribed in this document do not therefore relieve the pilot of his responsibilities of ensuring that any clearance issued by an air traffic control unit are safe in this respect, except when an IFR flight is vectored by radar." Nevertheless the Court of Inquiry examined this issue for days together. The concerned air traffic control personnel were put on the witness stand and subjected to a severe and intense interrogation, which went into the scope of their duties, their knowledge and understanding of the various provisions of ICAO documents relating to air traffic control, their professional competence, the clearance issued by them and so on.

In the face of this onslaught, the case would perhaps have gone quite adversely for air traffic control but for two individuals. The first, the erstwhile Controller of Aerodromes, Mumbai and the second, a very capable, intelligent and knowledgeable senior air traffic controller. The Controller of Aerodromes was convinced that the ATC Bombay was not at fault and stood firm and vowed to fight it out. The Senior Air Traffic Controller an Anglo-Indian gentleman was a very competent air traffic controller well versed in rules regulations and procedures concerning air traffic control. But more important, he possessed an extraordinary legal turn of mind. (I have mentioned elsewhere that air traffic controllers, generally do not possess the legal frame of mind). He was at that time posted at Calcutta Airport but was fielded by the Department to defend Air Traffic Control Mumbai. His brilliant exposition of the role of air traffic control and lucid delineation of the import and interpretation of ICAO rules were convincing. Air Traffic Control was exonerated. The Court of Inquiry made certain recommendations in respect of commencement of descent by pilots during bad weather conditions and during periods of darkness to obviate recurrence of such accidents. Air traffic controllers also became wary after that accident in issuing descent clearances to aircraft.

Another Damocles's sword hanging over the controllers' head is the unwelcome prospect of unwittingly making an error while working which could result in an 'nearmiss'. A nearmiss is technically a situation where the separation between two aircraft had broken down to the extent that there was danger of collision. The current term for such situation is however 'airprox' short for 'aircraft proximity', which refers to a situation in which the distance between aircraft as well as their relative positions and speed have been such that the safety of the aircraft involved may have been compromised. Airprox is classified as risk of collision, safety not assured, no risk of collision and risk not determined.

In actual practice however any reduction of the minimum prescribed separation between two aircraft is treated as a 'nearmiss' (or airprox) and investigated accordingly. For example, if it comes to light in a particular case that the separation between two aircraft had broken down to thirteen minutes from the required minimum separation of fifteen minutes, it is treated similar to a nearmiss and investigated to establish the causes for the reduction in separation, and more important, to take corrective measures to avoid recurrence of similar cases.

A nearmiss occurring in the course of his duty is a traumatic experience for a controller. It gives a deep shock to his moral sense and a severe below to his professional pride; 'shock to his moral sense' because the nearmiss could well have been a midair collision and a controller suffers inwardly in contemplation of the potential ghastly consequences of his error; 'blow to his professional pride' because in the controllers' profession a 'nearmiss' is considered equivalent to the original sin; his copy book has been permanently blotted and he carries the stigma for the rest of his carrier. It is never forgotten. Apart from such subjective ordeals he also suffers materially as his ratings are immediately suspended and he is not allowed to perform air traffic control duties till the conclusion of the investigation which normally takes months to complete. If the investigation reveals that he was blameworthy, appropriate action is taken against him and he is subjected to 're-training' before being allowed to perform air traffic control duties again.

Nearmisses (or airproxes) may take place on account of a variety of causes. They could of course take place due to carelessness or negligence on the part of the controller. Quite often they take place on account of coordination lapses when aircraft are transferred from one controller to another. Many an avoidable nearmiss has taken place due to improper or hasty 'take over, hand over' of watch. It has been mentioned earlier that a controller while 'taking over watch' must familiarise himself with the current traffic situation as well as other information regarding status of runways, navaids, weather etc and any slackness in this respect can result in a nearmiss.

Nearmisses can also take place on account of slips or oversight while working under conditions of stress. This could happen particularly under procedural control where it is easy for the controller to unwittingly lapse into an error. While calculating estimates, for instance, he could under the stress of the moment add up 28 minutes and 14 minutes, mentally as 52 minutes instead of 42 and this could easily be the cause of a nearmiss.

Or under sheer workload of having to handle very heavy traffic he may commit a blunder. However, very curiously instances of nearmisses occurring under conditions of heavy traffic is not very common. Perhaps this is because during periods of heavy traffic the controller works with utmost concentration and alertness. His mental faculties are keyed to the highest pitch. But during comparatively slack periods there may be a tendency on the part of the controller to drop his guard and this, too often results in a nearmiss.

Nearmisses could also take place due to extraneous causes, that is due to causes other than negligence, oversight or error on the part of the controller. They could take place on account of non-compliance, improper compliances of ATC clearances by the pilot. They could also take place on account of poor communications system; as for example ATC may have failed to receive information of an aircraft movement and when that aircraft enters his area, the controller would find to his consternation that this unknown aircraft is conflicting with another aircraft under his control and it is too late to take any remedial action. Or very rarely, he may realise that two aircraft are on collision course and may yet, be unable to issue appropriate clearances to avert the potential collision on account of inability to contact the concerned aircraft. A very nasty nearmiss of this type occurred within Chennai FIR during the year 1980.

The circumstances were as follows :

A Malaysian aircraft was bound for Madras from Kualalumpur at FL 350 on route B 466 (Fig. 4.2). This route B 466 is a very busy route as most of the flights between Southeast Asia and Middle-east/Eastern Europe follow this route which passes through Chennai. The route is particularly busy during periods of night in view of the curfew on night landings at most of the European Airports. The flights adjusts their timings so as to land at such airports after day break, which naturally involves flying over Indian Airspace during periods of night.

Below the Malaysian aircraft cruising at FL 350, there were other aircrafts at lower levels bound for airports in Europe or the Middle-East. The next higher level available for Westbound flights was FL 390 which was not occupied by any aircraft at that time (As per Rules of the Air, FLs 290, 330, 370 etc are applicable for Eastbound flights and FLs 310, 350, 390 etc are applicable for Westbound flights).*

Route B 466 along which the Malaysian aircraft was flying is crossed by another important route G 465 which runs from Bangkok to Colombo. The crossing point of these two routes falls within Chennai FIR and is designated as ATIDA. However, route G 465 had far less traffic than B 466.

There was a Qantas Airways aircraft flying along G 465 also at FL 350 bound for Colombo. The estimates of the Malaysian aircraft and the Qantas aircraft over ATIDA the crossing point of the routes were exactly the same. This kind of conflicts used to occur quite frequently as G 465 enters Chennai area from Rangoon area and B 466 enters from Kuala lumpur area and on the shoulders of ATC Chennai fell the responsibility of resolving these conflicts. The crossing point of the routes was only at a short distance from point of entry into Chennai area,

*The purpose is to provide separation between opposite direction flights; the traffic pattern is mostly East to West and West to East.

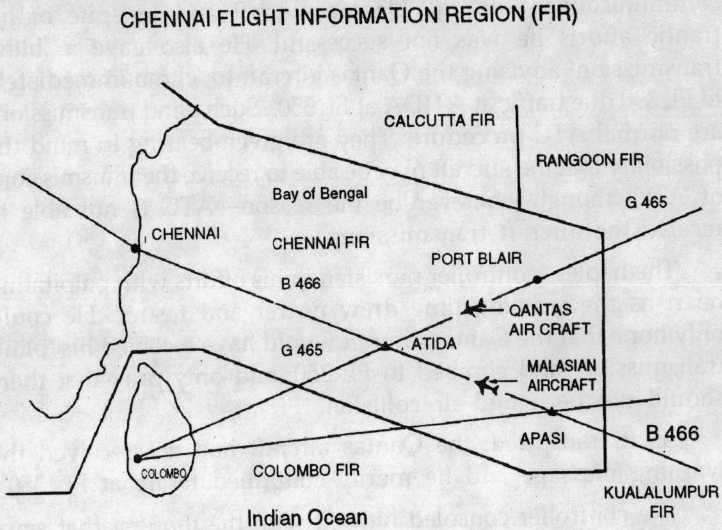

Fig. 4.2

which allowed ATC Chennai only a short period of time to act to resolve the potential collisions.

As soon as the controller became aware of the conflict, he acted with alacrity to advise the Malysian aircraft, with which he was in communication to climb to FL 390 to avoid conflict with the Qantas aircraft at FL 350. The Malaysian aircraft reported inability to climb to FL 390 presumably because he was too heavy on account of the weight of the fuel he was carrying.

It may again be mentioned here that long distance flights carry enormous amount of fuel and are therefore very heavy in the initial stages of the flight. This constrains them in climbing to higher levels. As the fuel gets progressively consumed, the aircraft become gradually lighter and prefer to climb to higher levels at which the fuel consumption is less.

The Malaysian aircraft was firm in its refusal to climb to FL 390 in spite of being informed of the conflicting traffic at FL 350. The aircraft could not be allotted any lower level as there were other aircraft occupying these levels at that time. So the only course open to the controller was to advise the other aircraft, to climb to FL 390. The controller tried to establish communication with the Qantas aircraft and in spite of his frantic afforts he was not successful. He also gave a 'blind transmission' advising the Qantas aircraft to 'climb immediately to FL 390 due traffic at ATIDA at FL 350'. Such blind transmissions are normal ATC procedure. They are given bearing in mind the possibility that the aircraft may be able to receive the transmissions of ATC, though-whatever be the reason—ATC is not able to receive the aircraft transmissions.

The hapless controller persisted in his efforts with palpitating heart as the crossing time drew nearer and nearer. He could only hope that the Qantas aircraft would have received his 'blind transmission' and climbed to FL 350, and only pray that there should not be a mid-air collision.

As it transpired, the Qantas aircraft had not received the warning message and he merily continued to fly at FL 350.

The controller consoled himself with the thought that since the Malaysian aircraft had been made aware of the other aircaft at the same level, he would keep a sharp watch and if necessary carry out avoiding manoeuvres in time if required. However as it actually happened, the Malaysian aircraft did sight the Qantas aircraft, but somewhat late, and a violent manoeuvre had to be carried out to avert a collision and in the process some passengers aboard that aircraft, were injured. After landing at Madras the pilot of the Malaysian aircraft filed a 'nearmiss' report. No such report was received from the pilot of the Qantas aircraft, then or later and it seems that the incident was not noticed by the pilot of the aircraft.

In the investigation that followed, the controller was fully absorbed of any blame in respect of the nearmiss as he had done everything in his power as per standard procedures to avoid the situation. This nearmiss incident attracted international attention and some foreign newspapers carried new items regarding that incident.

Problems of poor communications were something which I had to face during my years as a controller as also every other controller in India. While incidents of the above nature were rare, poor communications severely constrained us in our work and harassed us and robbed us of our precious time and concentration while handling traffic. Many a nearmiss in which the controller was held to blame was partly due to poor communications. Apart from poor communications, failure or malfunctioning of equipment like radio navigation facilities, radar and so on was quite common. The controller depends on these facilities for carrying out his job. When they fail and that also very suddenly while he is wrestling with traffic, he becomes terribly hamstrung in his efforts to discharge his duties. One can well imagine the plight of a controller, vectoring eight aircraft on the radar, when the equipment goes off suddenly and all the blips on the radar disappear. He is required to reconfigure the traffic by issuing appropriate clearances so that the required minimum separation as applicable under non-radar control is immediately provided. This is by no means an easy task. The controller has really to struggle and juggle and it is in these moments that his frustration reaches its peak.

In the event of something going amiss, no allowance or indulgence is normally granted to the controller for failure of equipment or malfunctioning of communication channels which might have indirectly contributed to the incident. On the other hand, the technical staff who are responsible for proper maintenance of the equipment and facilities are rarely, if ever penalised for failure or disruption of such facilities. The relationship between air traffic controllers and the technical personnel tends therefore to be hostile. The controllers feel that they have to hear the cross for the inefficiency of the technical personnel. The technical staff feel that the controllers are lording it over them. During my tours abroad I had guardedly tried to assess the relationship between controllers and technical personnel in other countries. While disruption or failure of equipment is not as endemic in the developed countries as in India (and even in the nations of the Middle East and South East Asia). I still got the feeling that in these countries also the relationship between controllers and technical staff were, in general not cordial.

Air traffic incidents and nearmisses take place not only in India, but in every other country that has an air traffic control. Volume of air traffic and consequent airspace congestion in most of the developed countries is of course much more than in India. For example while the number of movements handled by area Control Centre Mumbai was about 200,000 in 1995 the number of movements handled by the area control centre at New Hampshire in the United States of America which I had the opportunity to visit in 1995 was more than 1 million per year.

The number of nearmiss incidents or to use the latest term Airprox-Risk of Collision incidents in India during the last four years is given in the table below along with the total number of aircraft movements over India and the Indian FIRs during the same period.

Year	No. of Airprox-Risk of Collision Incidents
1994	17
1995	13
1996	13
1997	19

Year	Total No. of Aircraft Movements (Landing, Take off & Overflghts)
1993-94	540,000
1994-95	600,000
1995-96	688,000
1996-97	736,000
1997-98	823,000

It appears therefore that the number of incidents per 100,000 movements is actually showing a decrease in the last four years.

During my long career in air traffic control, providentially no nearmiss occurred. I say 'providentially' because as mentioned earlier even while exercising utmost care in one's work a lapse can unwillingly occur. It will be a very bold controller who can boast that he is above committing errors. I, for one, would not claim to have made no errors. The controller who has not made a single error in his work is still to be born. But these were generally either minor lapses without having serious implications for aircraft safety or they were detected and rectified before any untoward incident could occur. In a few instances where I had erred, the realization that I had commited an error came to my mind suddenly after a day or two later. It was as if the 'error' had lodged itself in the sub-conscious as an irritant and the sub-conscious was forced to eject it into my conscious mind to rid itself of the irritant. I do not know whether other controllers had similar experiences. I had never tried to find out.

I was not therefore subjected to any inquiry directed specifically into my shortcomings in the performance of air traffic control duties. The few inquiries in which I was called upon to give evidence were all in relation to other than purely air traffic incidents, like aircraft swinging of the runway, aircraft suffering damage due to bird hit and so on. But during my second posting at Chennai there was an occasion where a pilot felt that incorrect information had been given by me on a matter having the most serious implication for air safety.

The circumstances were as follows. One of the items of information that a controller is required to issue to a pilot is the current aerodrome pressure data. This is a vital piece of information. The altimeter which measures the height of the aircraft is based upon the principle of reduction of atmospheric pressure with altitude. For the altimeter to record correctly it is imperative that the datum pressure, which is the aerodrome pressure, be correctly set. Since the atmospheric pressure keeps on changing, it is necessary that the changes should be notified immediately to the pilot. In view of the importance of this data, whenever it is passed to the pilot it is 'read back', that is it repeated by him so that the controller can assure himself that it has been correctly received.

On that day, I was on duty at the approach radar. It was about ten O'clock in the morning and somewhat unusually the traffic was heavy on account of some airforce and nonscheduled movements. The approach frequency was bad the reception of the aircraft transmissions was very 'distorted', that is very difficult to make out. The flight in question was an Indian Airlines Being 737 coming to land at Chennai after taking off from Bangalore. The aircraft was 'handed over' to me by the area controller at about 50 nautical miles West of Chennai. In accordance with the routine procedure I passed the current weather information and the aerodrome pressure data, (technically termed the 'QNH') which was 1006 millibars at that time. I vectored the aircraft for runway 25, for which the approach was over the sea from East to West and at each stage of the descent passed the QNH as 1006 millibars. The reception on the frequency, as I have mentioned earlier was very bad and I had to strain myself to listen to and understand the aircraft transmissions. The traffic was also heavy which further increased my strain. After vectoring the Indian Airlines aircraft for an approach for runway 25, I handed over the aircraft to the tower controller at about 7 miles from the runway, when he reported runway in-sight.

About ten minutes after the aircraft had landed I was called up on telephone by the pilot of the Indian Airlines aircraft. The traffic had somewhat eased by that time and I took the call. The pilot was in a highly agitated mood and he accused me in a very excited tone of having wrongly passed the QNH as 1016 millibars. I remember telling him immediately that 'as sure as I am standing here and talking to you, I have passed you the QNH as 1006 millibars and not as 1016'. He was not convinced. But I stood my ground and remained firm as I was certain that I could not have passed incorrect QNH; very early in my career I had formed the habit of 'reading out' the QNH from the weather charts or the TV monitor and never, never pass it from memory.

The pilot's agitation was understandable. He had set the datum pressure of the altimeter as 1016 instead of the actual pressure of 1006 millibars. Under such conditions the altimeter would 'overread' by about 300 feet; that is if the actual altitude was 1000 feet, the altimeter would read as 1300 feet (conversely if the datum pressure was 1016 and it had been set wrongly as 1006, the altimeter would 'underead'). Since the weather was good at that time, the pilot had realized that the altimeter indication was not correct and had safely manoeuvred the aircraft visually to make a landing. A similar error under conditions for bad weather could have ended up in disaster.

As I have already mentioned there were other aircraft which were also handled by me at the same time as the Indian Airlines Boeing 737 from Bangalore. The Delhi airbus (also belonging to Indian Airlines) had landed just a few minute before the Bangalore flight. There was no complaint from any of them. All of them had noted the QNH correctly as 1006. But for some odd reason, the pilot of this particular aircraft had noted the QNH incorrectly.

In accordance with the usual procedure, I recorded the 'incident' in my logbook. The tape was replayed the next day and it revealed that I had passed the QNH as 1006, not once, but three times and all the three times the pilot had 'read back' as 1016. The question then arose as to why I did not correct the pilot when he had read back the QNH incorrectly. This had happened as the reception on the receiver was very distorted and I had hence failed to notice the wrong 'read back'. However a formal investigation was kept pending awaiting a written 'Air Traffic Incident Report' from the pilot.

But that report never came. The pilot perhaps thought that he could also be substantially blamed for the incorrect setting of the QNH. All other aircraft had correctly noted the QNH. The fault was with my receiver, not my transmitter. No aircraft had reported that my transmissions were not clear. Secondly the Area Controller who had handed over the aircraft to me must have passed the QNH and it is inconceivable that the QNH can jump by 10 millibars (from 1006 to 1016) within a few minutes. Even if I had passed the QNH wrongly as '1016' it should have been evident to the pilot that it cannot be correct. Whatever might have been the reason, no complaint in writing was made. The matter was dropped at that.

In the above instance, incorrect setting of the QNH went off without any adverse consequences. But there are a number of instances in the History of Aviation where incorrect setting of the QNH has resulted in accidents resulting in loss of lives and property. One of the first things to be noted in an aircraft crash is whether the altimeter had been properly set.

One such accident consequent upon wrong setting of the QNH occurred at Calcutta in the year 1965. As I remember, the concerned aircraft was a Pan American Being 707. It was landing on runway 01 R (Right) at Calcutta during conditions of rainy weather. The QNH was 995 millibars; that is the barometric pressure was low which is normal during rainy weather. As per the ICAO regulations at that time, QNH was required to be passed in 'millibars'. Now, there are three units for measurement of aerodrome pressure, millibars, inches and millimetres. Instead of millibars' the term 'hectopascals' is used now-a-days. Earlier types of aircraft had their altimeters calibrated in inches later type of aircraft, in millibars. Russian aircraft used millimetres for calibrating the altimeters. As per the ICAO regulations, *if so requested by the pilot,* it should be passed in inches. In any case the appropriate unit should be mentioned.

The controller had passed the QNH as 995 millibars, in accordance with the standard procedure, to the Pan American aircraft. Pan American were using the 'inches' scale for setting of their altimeters in those days. The pilot mistook '995 millibars' for '29.95 inches' and set his altimeter to 29.95 inches. Now 29.95 inches corresponds to a QNH of about 1014 millibars. The pilot had therefore, in effect set his altimeter to 1014 millibars. As already pointed out this would result in 'overreading' of the altimeter by about 570 feet; that is the pilot would think he is higher by about 570 feet than his actual height.

The weather was rainy with reduced visibility and low clouds. On account of the wrong setting and the pilot being under the impression that he was higher than he actually was, the aircraft undershot the runway and landed on the ground much before the beginning of the runway. Miraculously, it did not and up in a total crash thanks to the pilot's skill in handling the aircraft in a bizarre situation. Still about five persons were killed. The pilot and crew were safe.

The matter was investigated by a court of inquiry which came to the obvious conclusion that wrong setting of the QNH was the cause of the accident. This accident illustrates how a simple, even silly error could end in loss of precious human lives.

Another series of incidents which on the face of it are caused by lack of cautiousness on the part of the pilot but in which the air traffic control also gets unavoidably involved are incidents in which aircraft mistake one aerodrome for another and effect or try to effect a landing. This is not an unusual occurrence and is perhaps caused due to 'momentary disorientation'. It happens generally when two aerodromes (one of which is the intended destination) are close to each other like Chennai and Tambaram airfields, Mumbai and Juhu, Hyderabad and Hakimpet (an airforce aerodrome) and so on. Generally the runways at neighbouring aerodromes have almost similar orientations as the runway orientation is decided primarily by the direction of the surface wind; aircraft land and take-off *against* the wind and so while constructing an airport a study of the prevailing surface wind conditions in different seasons over a period of years is carried out and the runway is so constructed that for a major part of the year the surface wind will be favourable for landing and take-off. Since the prevailing surface wind conditions at aerodromes close to each other will be similar, runway orientations are also similar. Under these circumstances some other aerodrome is mistaken for the aerodrome of landing in an unwary if the pilot is unfamiliar with the destination aerodrome. Such an unexpected approach and landing can obviously be most dangerous; runway length may not be sufficient, some other aircraft may be landing or taking off, or there may be obstructions on the runway like cattle, vehicles, people working and so on.

In such incidents the air traffic control gets involved as question is raised as to how the aircraft was issued clearance to land at the destination aerodrome by the tower controller when it was not actually to land there, or how it was allowed to approach and land at the other aerodrome. (What was the tower controller doing when he could see an unknown aircraft approaching? Why did he not issue warning signals?)

One of the earliest of such incidents occurred sometime during the fifties when a BOAC aircraft (company's name was changed to British Airways in the early seventies), a Comet landed at Juhu aerodrome mistaking it for Mumbai (Santa Cruz) Airport. Juhu airfield is very close to Mumbai Airfield-about one and a half miles distance and has its own 'traffic circuit' and control tower. There appear to be no other instance anywhere else in the world of two airfields having separate control towers, with the traffic circuit of one practically within the traffic circuit of the other. Juhu is a much smaller airfield, though older than Mumbai Airport and its main East-West runway is only 3600 feet long. Due to proximity of the two airfields aircraft approaching to land at Mumbai Airport from the West quite frequently attempt to make a mistaken landing at Juhu (Fig 4.3). On account of this the use of runway 09 at Mumbai is avoided as far as possible.*

The comet aircraft which landed at Juhu providentially escaped without loss of lives or major damage to the aircraft. Some days later it was flown out of Juhu itself by Chief Pilot of the airlines, after it was stripped off of all fittings and so on to make it as light as possible.

Standard Operating Procedures comprising some twelve items of instructions have been issued which are required to be followed whenever runway 09 is used for a landing at Mumbai during day time. During those periods, Juhu tower is informed and it keeps a sharp watch and if the aircrafts heads for Juhu, during the final approach, Juhu fires a red catridge (which is a signal to the pilot meaning 'Notwithstanding any previous instruction do not land for the time being') and simultaneously alerts Mumbai Tower by means of a 'buzzer' specially provided for this purpose. 'Procedures when runway 09 is used for landing' is a very important thing in the training of tower controllers at Juhu.

When I was ATC Instructor at Mumbai, sometime in 1990, I was imparting training to a batch of freshly recruited aerodrome officer trainees (air traffic controllers) who were undergoing their 'ab-initio' training at the Civil Aviation Centre, Allahabad. (The training procedure for new air traffic controllers was that they would first undergo 4 months theoretical and simulator training in aerodrome control at the CATC, and then be positioned at any one of the four international airports for practical training where they would be expected to acquire their tower ratings before going back to the C.A.T.C. to complete the remaining part of their training). I explained to the trainees the operating procedures that were to be observed whenever runway 09 is intended to be used for aircraft landing. On the spur of the moment I decided to have a practical demonstration of the procedures. We were using runway 27 at that time and there was an airbus aircraft approaching over the Arabian Sea, from

* Runway 09 at Mumbai Airport is being provided with ILS as part of the Modernisation Project. It will help to eliminate such mistaken landings.

the west. I decided to give runway 09 for landing which would be highly acceptable to him as he could come in straight and land and save about thirty miles of extra flight and about ten minutes time than if he were to land on runway 27. (Fig. 4.3)

Fig. 4.3 : Mumbai and Juhu Airfields

I advised the approach radar controller accordingly. There was only one other traffic at that time, a Gulfair Tristar taxing out for departure from runway 27 which I had to delay much to his chagrin which he expressed volubly.

I gave effect to the items of the Standard Operating Procedure one by one explaining each step. We could see the aircraft on long final of runway 09. As per the operating procedures the approach (radar) controller does not hand over the aircraft till he is very close to the runway but keeps the aircraft with himself so that in the event it appears that the aircraft is veering toward Juhu as seen on the radar, the approach radar controller could warn him immediately.

We solemnly watched the aircraft approaching. *And as we were watching I saw the aircraft turning left away from the final approach of runway 09 of Mumbai and at that instant came the warning buzzer from Juhu tower.* The Juhu tower controller called up on the direct telephone and excitedly told us that 'airbus trying to land at Juhu.' I immediately advised the approach radar controller to warn the aircraft. The approach controller warned the aircraft but the pilot stated that he was heading for runway 09 of Mumbai only. And as we watched the aircraft adjusted its heading and landed at Mumbai.

I talked to the approach controller after the aircraft had landed and parked in its stand. The approach controller was satisfied with the statement of the pilot that he was aligned for runway 09 all the time and accordingly no 'air traffic incident' had occurred. The whole thing had passed off alright and perhaps the approach controller felt that it would be wiser not a raise a ruckus over affair. This is a general attitude of controllers; avoid making a report or complaint if possible. An investigation can more often than not recoil on the controller. The Inquiry Officer after probing through the records, laid down procedures and so on quite frequently manages to find out 'some action' that the controller could have taken that would have averted the incident. I also did not press the issue for the same reason though my strong feeling was that the aircraft had at least momentarily mistaken Juhu for Mumbai. The Juhu controller to whom I spoke was also firm that the aircraft was making for Juhu. He did not also make a report.

The earliest instance in my career of approach at a wrong aerodrome took place in the very year of my joining as a controller at Chennai Airport though not in my watch. An Indian Air Force Dakota was proceeding from Hyderabad to Tambaram and was estimating Tambaram at about 5 O'clock in the evening. It was handled at first by Madras Approach and then handed over to Tambaram Tower when it reported Tambaram in sight. Chennai Airport and Tambaram airfield have a set of parallel runways of orientation Northwest/ Southeast (Runways 12/30). The aircraft apparently cleared for runway 12 at Tambaram, made an approach for runway 12 at Madras. The alert controller noted the aircraft approaching and quickly comprehending the situation acted promptly. He immediately informed Tambaram as he had no contact with the aircraft himself and also fired a red catridge which as already mentioned is a signal to the pilot conveying 'notwithstanding any previous instruction, do not land for the time being'. The aircraft abandoned the approach and subsequently landed at Tambaram. The controller, normally a placid person was really shaken up.

The last of such incidents in my career occurred at Coimbatore Aerodrome as late as in the year 1994. It was the inaugural flight of an 'Airtaxi Operator'. The aircraft, a Boeing 737 had with great fanfare taken off from Mumbai for Coimbatore airfield. This airfield is situated close to an airforce airfield called Sulur which is located about 5 miles east of it. Both the airfields have runways of similar orientation 05/23 that is northeast to southwest. The pilot of the Boeing 737 was not familiar with Coimbatore and this was his first flight to that airport. It was about 10 O'clock in the morning when he approached Coimbatore. He reported 'airfield in sight' but apparently had sighted Sulur airfield and mistaken that for Coimbatore. After some time he reported 'final' and the Coimbatore controller issued the landing clearance without noticing that the aircraft was nowhere in sight. The control tower of Sulur suddenly saw an aircraft, apparently from nowhere making a landing on their runway'! One can only imagine the reaction of the passengers of this inaugural flight when they were sheepishly informed by the airlines staff that they had landed at the wrong airfield!

There was a curious event during my watch when I was working as approach radar controller at Madras when I suspect that an aircraft had mistaken Tambaram airfield for Chennai Airport when he was being vectored by me. The flight in question was an Indian Airlines scheduled flight from Calcutta to Chennai. The flight was estimating Chennai at about 12 noon and it was slack period and there was only one other aircraft handled by me at that time. I was vectoring the Calcutta flight for a 'visual approach' runway 07 for which I had to take the aircraft about 10 miles west of Chennai Airport and then give the equivalent of an (almost) 'U' turn to put it on the final approach of runway 07 (Fig 4.4) to settle at about 8 miles from the runway. Just as the aircraft passed position 'P' shown in the figure, the pilot told me 'we have crossed your runway'. This message gave me a jolt. The aircraft was actually heading away from the runway and there could be no question of 'crossing' the runway. Had I made a mistake? Had I perhaps misidentified' the aircraft? (Misidentification means wrongly correlating a blip with a particular aircraft. This can be highly dangerous as navigational instructions would be issued to one aircraft presuming it to be some other. Misidentification is one of the greatest and most serious blunders that a radar controller could commit. Controllers are aware of this and such blunders are very rare. But it could not be misidentification; there were only two on the radarscope and they were well apart, to preclude any such possibility. Puzzled and disconcerted, I did not respond to the pilot's comment but continued my vectoring.

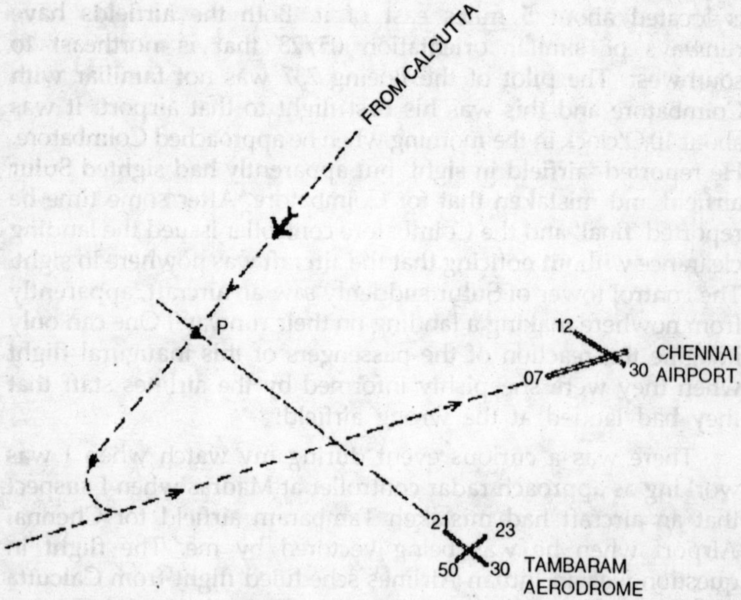

Fig. 4.4. Chennai Airport and Tambaram Aerodrome Vectoring for Runway 07 Chennai Airport.

As I issued the instruction to 'turn left heading one zero zero to intercept the localizer at eight miles from touchdown' it suddenly struck me as to why the pilot had made that comment. *He had apparently mistaken Tambaram runway 12 for his runway.* As can be seen from the figure at position 'P' he would just have crossed the final approach of Tambaram runway 12 which he had mistaken for Madras runway 07 and thought that the controller was taking him out when he should have been turned inwards to settle on the final approach.

This may appear to be far fetched but it is fully within the realms of possibility. Under radar vectoring the pilot places himself in the hands of the controller as it were and while he may cross check his position from time to time, he is generally satisfied to leave it to the controller to guide his aircraft. In the present case, the pilot was being vactored for a 'visual approach' runway 07 and he was looking out expecting to get his runway in sight. He saw the runway and while he was anticipating that the controller would give him a left turn to align his aircraft with the runway he found that he was allowed to cross his runway (as he thought) and drift away; that provoked him to make the comment that 'We have crossed your runway'.

Having understood this I relaxed. I waited for the aircraft to settle on the final approach of runway 07 of Chennai and then I told him 'Seven miles from touchdown Report Madras runway 07, I say again, Madras runway 07 in sight.' I stressed and repeated the words 'Madras runway 07' to indicate that I had understood his mistaking of Tambaram runway 12 for 07 of Madras.

Very recently, that is on 2nd June 97 a Saudia Airlines B 747 bound for Madras from Riyadh landed instead at Tambaram Air Force airfield. The aircraft which had about 350 persons on board including the crew was approaching Chennai Airport at about 7 O'clock in the morning for runway 07 (Fig. 4.4). The pilot opted to make a visual approach instead of an instrument approach and reported final runway 07 to Chennai Tower. The Tower Controller while issuing landing clearance, informed the pilot that "We have not got you in sight". The pilot of the aircraft which was actually on final runway 05 of Tambaram realised the mistake only after touching down. He jammed the brakes, bursting all the tyres but managed to bring the aircraft safely to a halt on the short runway of about 4800 feet.

Good fortune and quick reaction on the part of the pilot averted what could have resulted in a horrendous accident. That such an incident should take place in this age when hitech and sophisticated airborne and ground equipment are available, highlights the fact that the 'human factor' is still very important in aircraft operations.

Four days later the aircraft was flown out of Tambaram airfield to Chennai Airport. An almost identical scenario as in the incident of a comet aircraft landing at Juhu airfield forty years ago was reenacted. A very senior pilot of the airlines was deputed to carry out the take off from Tambaram. The aircraft was stripped bare to reduce its weight and only minimum fuel necessary to reach Chennai Airport was carried. The pilot chose runway 12 the longer runway of about 5800 feet for take off. He waited for over three hours for the easterly wind to set in which would give him some headwind component while taking off reducing the length of runway required.

While one may understand the mistaking of one aerodrome for another when they are closely situated and have runways of similar orientation, there have been cases where such mistaking had occurred when the aerodromes were at a considerable distance from each other. One such incident which took place as in 1993 involved a Boeing 737 on scheduled flight from Mumbai to Ranchi, which had approached over Jamshedpur aerodrome at a low altitude though that aerodrome was well beyond its route. It was dusk time and the aircraft climbed up and subsequently landed at Ranchi. It appears again to be a case of mistaking one aerodrome for another. The matter was reported by ATC Jamshedpur to the Air Safety Directorate Authorities for investigation.

It may appear from all that had been said earlier that a controllers job is merely 'preventive' and that he has no positive contribution to make. While this is by and large true, there are still occasions where a controller could and does afford positive support and assistance to a pilot; on such occasions the controller gets a deep sense of satisfaction and achievement.

Such opportunity arises during conditions of bad weather when the controller can provide valuable assistance to a pilot by vectoring the aircraft clear of weather with the help of his radar. Under radar control the controller assumes the responsibility for the 'navigation' of the aircraft. Navigation is the process of managing or directing the course of an aircraft (or a ship) using maps and instruments; and it is of course distinct from the process of 'flying' the aircraft. During earlier times navigators were part of the crew of an aircraft and they performed the function of 'navigation' while the pilot 'flew' the aircraft. With the introduction of increasingly sophisticated navigation equipment, the function of navigators on board an aircraft became redundant and gradually they were dispensed with. Pilots performed both the functions. But under radar control, as already mentioned, when 'tactical vectoring' is exercised it is the controller who decides upon the path the aircraft is to follow and accordingly issues appropriate headings to the pilot. The pilot flies the aircraft in accordance with the headings given by the radar controller. During periods of bad weather while using primary radar this can turn out to be a very demanding task for the controller. Primary radars, unlike secondary radars 'reflect' the 'weather' also; that is on the radar screen areas of heavy weather are presented as opaque patches. While this is very useful to know the areas under bad weather, they make vectoring difficult by obliterating the blip of the aircraft. The 'weather' on a radar screen can be reduced by appropriate devices but not entirely eliminated. While all this enable the controller to vector the aircraft clear of the 'weather', it is yet a very demanding task requiring high concentration to keep the aircraft blip within his view as it can easily be lost to view in the background of patches (weather) all around.

Pilots set a high degree of appreciation for such guidance and assistance when provided. They invariably express their thanks for the assistance given, particularly when the vectoring is carried out under very demanding conditions. This is a rewarding moment for the controller.

I had vectored many an aircraft on primary radar after first acquiring my radar rating at Calcutta in the year 1972; I had vectored aircraft at Calcutta during the monsoon season; I had vectored aircraft a Chennai during periods of cyclonic storms. I had vectored aircraft at Mumbai Airport during monsoon. But still one particular vectoring which I carried out at Madras is still firmly etched in my memory.

The rainy season prevails at Chennai during the months of October, November and December when the Northeast, monsoon (or as the meteorologists call it 'retreat of the Southwest monsoon') is active. During such periods, depressions form in the Bay of Bengal which intensify as they move westward towards the coast often developing into a cyclone, and adjoining regions experience continual heavy rain during such times. The winds are strong and blow from the north east and gradually become easterly. They are thus favourable for runway 25 of Chennai Airport, that is for an approach from over the Bay of Bengal. (Fig 4.5) This runway was not equipped with any landing aids in those days as the designated 'instrument runway was runway 07, that is physically the same runway but approach from the opposite direction towards the sea. The reason for choosing runway 07 as the instrument runway was that for the major part of the year the surface wind was favourable for that runway. Ironically the winds were strongest during the cyclonic periods necessitating use of runway 25. In these circumstances the radar was of immense assistance to aircraft approaching to land at Madras.

We were in the midst of a developing cyclonic storm at Chennai. Weather was bad and there was intermittent rain. I was on duty on the approach radar and it was about midnight. The radar screen was cluttered with weather patches. The Indian Airlines Delhi airbus was delayed and it was approaching to land at Chennai. Runway in use for 25 and I offered radar vectoring to the aircraft. The pilot however initially opted to 'do his own navigation'. But after some time he himself sought radar help. The aircraft was actually somewhat east of his track having gone there in the process of the pilot trying to avoid the weather. I took over for radar vectoring for runway 25. The aircraft was about 30 miles north-north east of Madras Airport.

The situation was somewhat tricky. The approach of runway 25 was heavily cluttered but there was a 'gap' north of the final approach of the runway at about seven miles. I had to bring the aircraft through this gap and turn him on sharply on to the final approach. I could not afford to allow him to get into the clutter, both for the safety of the aircraft and for fear of 'losing' the blip. The aircraft had to be manoeuvred through the narrow gap and the final turn had to be timed accurately; if not the aircraft would not settle on the final approach track and in the prevailing weather conditions there was little chance that the pilot would sight the runway, align the aircraft properly and effect a landing.

Radar vectoring is not merely a game of skill but something of an art also. The reactions of pilots to instructions given by the controllers vary and a good controller takes note of this. For example, certain pilots, mostly of international flights fully read back the instructions given by the controller word for word in slow measured tones and then only execute the turn. Others read back the instructions faster and then execute the turn. Some

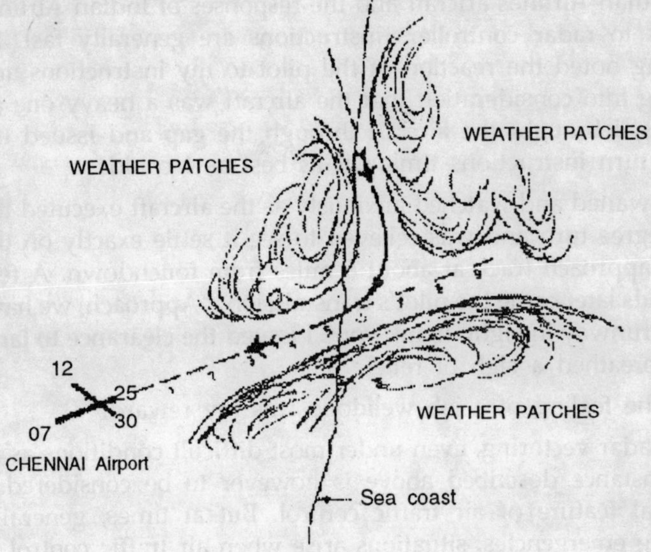

Fig. 4.5 : Vectoring for Runway 25-Chennai Airport

others may just read back only vital portions of the instructions for example if the radar controller instructs him to 'Turn right heading two four zero to intercept the localizer at eight miles from touchdown' he may merely respond laconically as 'right, heading two four zero' and then execute the turn.

These different types of reactions may result in differences of a few seconds only between the time the clearances are issued and the time they are actually executed and are not of much consequence for normal vectoring. But at critical phases of vectoring, particularly during the final turn to align on the final approach track these few seconds do matter. A good controller instinctively gets the 'sense' of the pilot's response in the pilot's reactions to the initial vectors given and then taking into account times the final turn accordingly.

In the incident that I am describing it was essential that the timing of the last turn on final approach should be perfect, considering that the aircraft was 'attacking' the final approach track at right angles at a distance of about 7 miles at an altitude of about two thousand feet. However the aircraft concerned was an Indian Airlines aricraft and the responses of Indian Airlines pilots to radar controllers instructions are generally fast. So having noted the reaction of the pilot to my instructions and taking into consideration that the aircraft was a heavy one an airbus, I brought the aircraft through the gap and issued the final turn instructions timing it as best as I could.

I waited and watched anxiously as the aircraft executed the 90 degree turn and was relieved to see it settle exactly on the final approach track at about 6 miles from touchdown. A few seconds later came the pilot's transmission : 'Approach, we have your runway in sight, thank you'. I issued the clearance to land and breathed a sigh of relief.

The feeling of a job welldone was my reward.

Radar vectoring, even under most difficult conditions as in the instance described above is however to be considered a normal feature of air traffic control. But at times, generally during emergencies, situations arise when air traffic control is called upon to deal with extraordinary situations calling for initiative, original thinking and boldness. Two such incidents still linger in my mind.

The first of these happened at Calcutta in the year 1972. In the aftermath of the Indo-Pak war, one DC6 of call sign 'Red Cross' was operating regularly between Calcutta and Dhaka. What exactly was the nature of this operation was not clear but it was said to be in the nature of a mercy mission under the aegis of the United Nations.

On one such flight the aircraft was coming from Dhaka to Calcutta. It was during the early weeks of the Southwest monsoon maybe late June or early July. It was about half past five in the evening. I was on duty at the approach radar position.

The aircraft called me up a few minutes after taking off from Dhaka. Dhaka is close to Calcutta, only about 125 miles and the flying time for a DC6 from Dhaka to Calcutta is just about 30 minutes. There was hardly any traffic at that time-only one other aircraft, an Indian Airlines Fokker Friendship coming from the west. The weather was not bad though it was monsoon time. So I had not switched on my radar and was applying procedural control for handling the traffic. The runway-in-use was 19 and it was quite convenient to work using procedural control at Calcutta whenever the runway-in-use was 19, which happened most of the time.

The Red Cross DC6 had climbed to and was maintaining 8000 feet (FL 80). I passed the weather and other routine information and asked him to call me again when he wished to descend from FL 80. When the aircraft did not request for descent clearance, even when it was just a few minutes short of the ETA (estimated time of arrival) I called him up. The pilot replied that he was flying in weather and would ask for descent after some time.

I waited for some more time. In bad weather it was quite usual for aircraft to deviate from their path to avoid the weather and get delayed in the process. I was not therefore, at that time unduly worried about the delay.

After a few minutes the pilot reported that his navigation instruments were unreliable and he was not sure of his position. I switched on the radar immediately and advised the Red Cross DC 6 to maintain level 80 and to 'standby'. The other aircraft which was coming from the west, the Indian Airlines Fokker asked for descent and I cleared him to FL 90, giving a standard separation of 1000 feet from the DC 6.

After switching on, it takes about two to three minutes for the radar to get ready for use. I peered into the radar screen to know the position of the Red Cross DC 6 but could not locate any blip which could correspond to that aircraft (which of course I would 'identify' before giving any radar service) I called up the pilot who again repeated that his position was lost due to unreliable instruments. I asked him to maintain level 80 and searched assiduously for the blip. There were a few patches of scattered weather but no blip could be seen.

At this juncture the pilot made a curious transmission; "Approach, I do not know our position, but we have just crossed a huge airfield". Since the only airfield close to Calcutta Airport is Barrackpore Aerodrome, an Indian Air Force Airfield, which is located to the north-north west of Calcutta at about 10 miles, I thought that the pilot was referring to that airfield. (The pilot could not have been referring to Calcutta itself as

In circumstances such as this, there is one equipment called the VHF/DF (Very High Frequency/Direction Finder) which is of considerable help. The earlier version of this equipment called the AD 200 was available at Calcutta. This instrument installed just by the side of the radar controllers' desk automatically indicates the bearing of an aircraft whenever the aircraft's transmitter is activated. That is, when the pilot of an aircraft activates his (VHF) transmitter by switching it on, the bearing (that is, the direction in terms of the compass) of the aircraft is automatically indicated by the VHF DF. The instrument we had in Calcutta was in analogue form, with a dial and pointer, the pointer indicating the direction of the aircraft. (In later more sophisticated models, the indication is in digital form). This instrument can be set on either of two modes; In one mode it indicates the direction of the aircraft from the airport (bearing) and in the other mode it indicates the track the aircraft must follow to reach the airport-obviously the reciprocal of the bearing (Fig 4.6). Generally it is kept in the latter mode to enable aircraft to be advised their track to the airport when so requested by them.

CALCUTTA AND DHAKA FLIGHT INFORMATION REGIONS (FIRS)

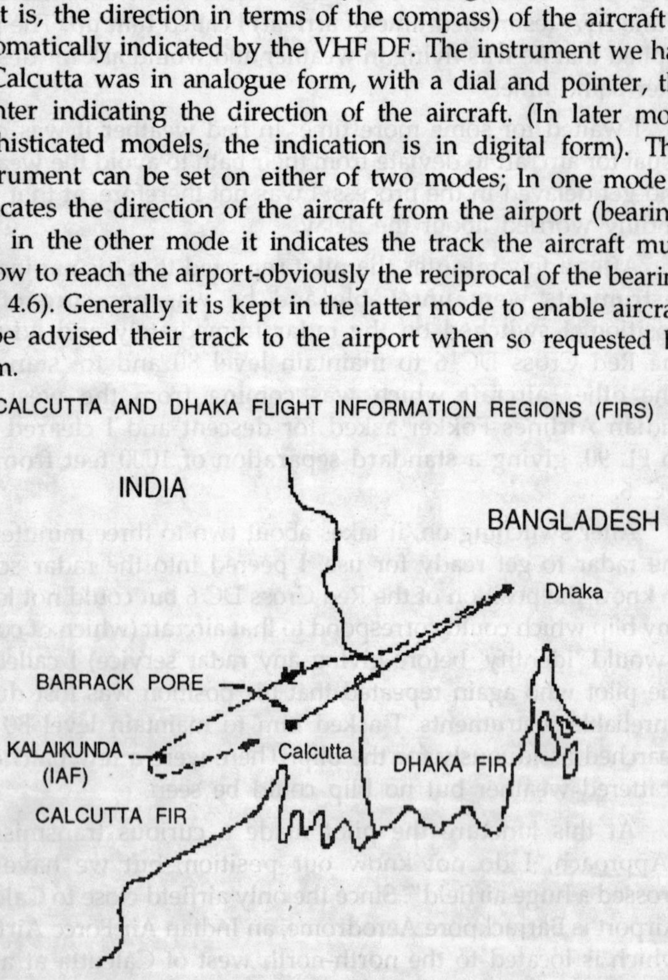

Fig. 4.6

Since the Red Cross DC 6 was not 'seen' on radar but was in communication, the AD 200 would indicate its bearing from the airport So I asked the pilot of the DC 6 to 'transmit for a bearing'. This means 'switch on your (VHF) transmitter and keep it on for some time'. It was necessary for the transmission to be maintained for about ten seconds for it takes the needle that amount of time to settle.

The pilot complied. I peered at the dial of the AD 200. The needle did not settle on any particular direction or bearing but it kept 'hunting' between 280 and 220 degrees. The 'red light' also did not burn. This is a lamp provided just below the dial of the AD 200. It lights up when the signal strength of tne aircraft's transmission is sufficiently high and indicates that the reading shown is reliable. If it does not light up, it indicates that the reading may not be reliable.

I asked the aircraft to 'transmit again for a bearing'. The reaction of the needle was the same-hunting between 220 and 280 with the red lamp not burning.

This was very surprising. Bearing 220/280 means that the aircraft is somewhere southwest to west of Calcutta. But since there was still no blip on the radar and I had nothing also to go by, I told the pilot to steer 070 degrees that is steer east northeast though not without considerable trepidation as I was taking the risk of leading the aircraft into Bangladesh territory by giving an easterly heading (based upon the indication of the AD 200 that the aircraft was west to southwest of Calcutta).

The aircraft acknowledged and confirmed after some time that his heading was 070. I asked him to 'transmit for a bearing' every two minutes. The needle was still fluctuating around about 250 degrees though the movement of the needle was becoming more and more brisk. A few minutes later the bearing was steady on 255 and the red lamp came on. That meant that the signal strength was increasing aircraft was coming closer. With full confidence now I kept giving him appropriate headings as per the indication on the AD 200. A few minutes later a blip appeared on the radar screen at about 35 miles west southwest of Calcutta Airport heading for Calcutta.

I identified it as the Red Cross DC 6. From there it was easy to vector the aircraft to Calcutta for a safe landing

What had presumably happened was that the aircraft had misnavigated due to its instruments not functioning properly and had passed north of Calcutta. The 'huge airfield' that the pilot was referring to, was obviously Kalaikunda airfield-an Indian Air Force Airfield which is located west southwest of Calcutta at a distance of about 70 miles.

The incident described above shows how the air traffic control could assist aircraft in trouble. A different type of incident took place during my posting at Mumbai, when air traffic control was called upon to assist an aircraft which was facing an unusual type of situation. The incident concerned an Air Lanka aircraft which had taken off from Karachi for Mumbai during June 1989. The aircraft on its first contact with area control, Mumbai reported that it was having some problem and required to land on a dry runway.

At that time I was in charge of the training of the controllers at Mumbai Airport and was not carrying out routine ATC duties. Still, since I happened to be in the area control at the time that the request was received from the aircraft, I took it upon myself to assist and guide the duty controllers in the handling of this unusual request.

We could not fully comprehend the nature of the engineering problem that the aircraft was facing. Controllers are taught to deal with aircraft emergencies but do not have, nor is it possible to have knowledge of every aspect of aircraft technology. On subsequent exchanges with the Air Lanka aircraft we gathered that it had some kind of 'flaps' problem and that it specifically required to make a landing on a dry runway only.

Generally any problem with the flaps indicate that the aircraft would have some constraint in slowing down after touchdown and so under such contingencies may be expected to 'consume' more than the normal distance for landing. So in such cases the longest runway available at an airport is given for the landing of the aircraft. Bombay Airport had a runway of length of 11,500 feet and a boeing 737 normally requires not more than 7000 feet. The runway length would therefore have been ample but for the express stipulation 'dry runway'. A very unusual requirement.

It was the month of June and the monsoon was very active at that time. Mumbai, was under the spell of the monsoon with continual showers and the runways were fully wet.

We considered the situation. We ascertained from the aircraft that the endurance was about 2 hours-that is the fuel on board will last for 2 hours of normal flying. We ran through the list of airports where the Air Lanka aircraft could possibly land. Ahmedabad Airport would have been ideal but it was also in the grip of the monsoon and in any case it could not be considered as the runway there was under some repairs at that time. Bangalore reported that the monsoon was active over their airfield and Nagpur was considered and dropped on account of the distance and possibility of weather closing in. Chennai weather was bright and sunny as Chennai is not affected much by the southwest monsoon but again Chennai was too far away and the aircrafts fuel condition may become critical if diverted to that airport. Pune was close to Mumbai and though it was an airforce airfield we were confident that the Indian Air Force Authorities would accept the aircraft if we requested them, but Pune was also in the throes of the monsoon. Further Pune was not a 'customs' airfield. Since the aircraft was coming from Karachi, on landing it had to undergo customs clearance formalities. While Ahmedabad, Chennai, Bangalore had customs clearance facilities, Pune did not have the same.

We then looked at Hyderabad; Long runway, customs facilities available and not too far from Mumbai about 320 miles. We contacted ATC Hyderabad, who reported that the weather was good and the controller on duty stated unequivocally that there appeared to be no possibility of weather deterioration. We decided to advise the aircraft to divert to Hyderabad.

In taking this decision there was one aspect we had to consider. On the normal direct route from Mumbai to Hyderabad, the 'restricted area' of Pune was situated. (Fig 4.7) These are airspaces reserved for the use of airforce flights and

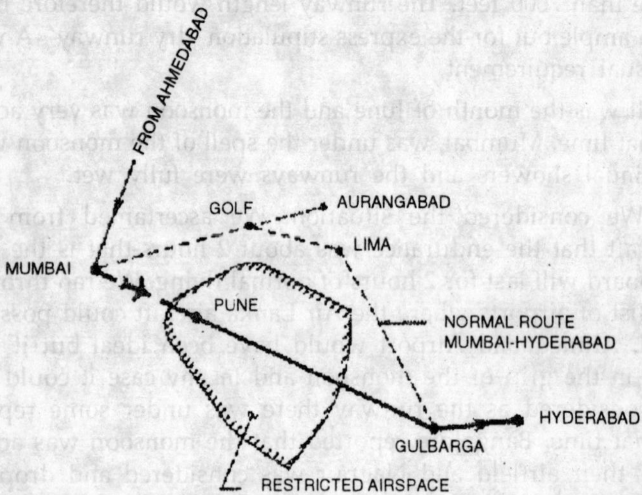

Fig. 4.7 : Mumabi-Hyderabad Routing

civil flights are not normally permitted to overfly these areas except with the permission of the airforce authorities, controlling these airspaces. The other route from Mumbai to Hyderabad avoiding the Pune restricted area was much longer. We were naturally anxious for the aircraft to complete its flight as early as possible both from the apprehension that the weather may deteriorate and also on account of the fuel position.

We contacted ATC Pune and explained the position and sought their permission for the Air Lanka flight to fly through their area to Hyderabad. In less than 2 minutes the permission was granted. This was evidence of high understanding and cooperation on the part of ATC Pune. It has to be understood that in giving permission ATC Pune would have to 'clear a path' for this aircraft, in terms of suitable dispositioning their flights operating in that area at that time. Generally in emergencies there is very high degree of understanding and cooperation between ATC units regardless of nationality or other considerations (except when ATC decisions are made the subject of extraneous considerations).

We advised the Air Lanka aircraft to proceed and land at Hyderabad. We gave him full details of Hyderabad airfield, runway orientation, length, navigation facilities and frequencies and so on as it would not have been in the mind of the pilot to land at Hyderabad and he would therefore not 'briefed' himself accordingly. Still the pilot would be carrying with him the ubiquitous 'Airway Manual' which would give him all the required information about Hyderabad.

During all this planning, nearly 15 to 20 minutes must have passed. The aircraft was approaching Mumbai. We calculated the remaining endurance as about a hour and forty minutes. Since the flying time to Hyderabad would be about 50 minutes for a Boeing 737 that would provide a margin of 50 minutes of fuel for safety which was quite comfortable.

But after the aircraft had set course for Hyderabad and changed over to ATC Pune, on query we were informed by the ATC that the aircraft had given an ETA (estimated time of arrival) Hyderabad, based on a flying time of not 50 minutes, but I hour and 15 minutes. We thought that it was a mistake but on further query ATC Pune told us that the aircraft had reported inability to maintain normal speed and had therefore descended to about 20,000 feet and was cruising at a much reduced speed of about 280 knots. This was probably on account of the flaps problem. Not only the flying time was being increased, fuel position was also giving concern as jet aircraft consume much more fuel at lower altitudes than at higher altitudes.

We were very anxious and were in constant touch with Hyderabad, asking the ATC again and again "How is your weather?" They assured us that the weather was good, and that they had stopped all departures and arrivals from their airfield. (This is a normal precaution taken in such circumstances to avoid the possibility of the runway getting blocked by some other aircraft due to some mishap like tyre burst and so on).

The Air Lanka Boeing 737 made a safe landing at Hyderabad. We breathed a deep sigh of relief. All is well that ends well, where our job is concerned.

The Air Lanka pilot contacted Air Traffic Control. Mumbai immediately upon landing and expressed his warm appreciation of our help. "The Times of India" Mumbai carried a news item on this incident which is reproduced below.

BOEING'S CRISIS IN BOMBAY SKIES

By a Staff Reporter

Bombay, June 30

The Bombay air traffic controllers were put to test on Thursday morning when an Air Lanka Boeing 737 from Karachi with 113 passengers on board was unable to land at the airport.

At 10 a.m. yesterday when the aircraft was coming into approach under the command of Captain Gunuwartane, its anti-skid mechanism became inoperative and the flaps got stuck.

Under these conditions the aircraft had to land on a dry runway. Yesterday following the heavy rains here the runway was wet. The commander at first thought of flying to Madras but decided against it because the fuel might run out.

A tense drama followed. As the Boeing could not hold for a long time the controllers had to quickly direct it to an alternative airfield.

Ahmedabad airport was considered but was dropped because the runway was under repair. Pune and Nagpur were eliminated because they were unsuitable for operational reasons.

After Capt. Gunuwartane was cleared to proceed to Hyderabad, Bombay ATC spent an anxious one hour until word reached that he had landed safely.

Air Lanka officials were all praise for the efficient handling of the crisis. "They did a superb job," an airline official told this paper.

I shall end this chapter with a description of another incident involving an aircraft in emergency which a lighter side.

It happened at Gaya aerodrome during June or July 1975. Earlier to 1969, Gaya Aerodrome was for a long time an international alternate for Calcutta Airport, that is flights which by reason of weather could not land at Calcutta, diverted to

Gaya. But after 1969 Gaya ceased to be an alternate aerodrome and its importance diminished and by 1975 even the bi or weekly Indian Airlines Viscount flights from Calcutta were discontinued. Gaya had become an almost idle aerodrome but for the flights of the Bihar State Government, which kept flitting between Patna and Gaya.

The Aerodrome Officer, Gaya was sitting in the verandah of his official residence at Gaya aerodrome roundabout dusk on that June evening. The calm of the evening was broken by the noise of an aircraft. As the Aerodrome Officer looked up he saw a small executive jet aircraft flying at low altitude over the aerodrome. This was surprising as he had no intimation regarding any flight to Gaya at that time. He realised immediately that this was an aircraft in some kind of emergency trying to land at Gaya. He could not make any attempt to contact the aircraft as the ATC was closed at that time. He at once issued instructions to open and activate the control tower. Meanwhile other residents of the aerodrome had come out on observing the aircraft.

By this time the aircraft had descended further and was seen approaching to land on the runway. As the Aerodrome Officer and the other watched, the aircraft landed on the runway. Fortunately the runway was clear of cattle or other obstructions.

The aircraft came to a halt on the runway. It was a small executive jet aircraft and from the markings it could be seen that it belonged to a foreign state. The Aerodrome Officer and others went in the jeep to the aircraft to find out to whom the aircraft belonged and why it had landed at Gaya. As they approached the aircraft the occupants were alighting and it was evident that they were foreign nationals.

Subsequently it was revealed that the executive jet belonged to one of the oil rich Middleast States. The Minister for Petroleum was on his way to Dhaka to discuss matters connected with the supply of petroleum products to Bangladesh; and that the aircraft had run out of fuel and had therefore made an emergency landing at Gaya aerodrome !

The occupants of the aircraft had to cool their heels at Gaya aerodrome for three or four days as the type of fuel that the aircraft required was not available at Gaya but had to be brought from somewhere else !

The various episodes that I have described in this chapter are but a few of many similar ones, that had occurred during the course of my long career. Many of them are forgotten or have been relegated to the depths of my subconscious. The few that I have narrated here have been permanently etched in my memory. Why they have been retained to the exclusion of other similar incidents or why I have considered apt to describe them only I cannot say. I feel however that these incidents portray well the trauma and drama of an almost unknown profession.

5

Mid-Air Collision Over Charkhi-Dadri

Twelfth of November 1996 was an unhappy day for civil aviation; that day witnessed a midair collision between two huge aircraft over the township of Charkhi Dadri, about 40 nautical miles (74 m) west of Delhi Airport resulting in the death of all 349 persons on board the two aircraft. The horrendous event took place at about 6. 40 P.M. Within minutes of the occurrence of the collision the news spread fast and wide. It dominated all other newsevents on the BBC TV channel. Air traffic controllers of India were seen and heard on that channel giving their comments on the collision and related matters. The Government on India immediately made public whatever information was available at that time to contain conjecture and speculation as to the causes of the collision.

The horrifying dimensions of the tragic event infused a sense of shock, regret and sympathy for the innocent and unfortunate victims of the tragedy and their near and dear ones.

Even during the early days of flying, even when it was still in the pioneering stage when there was hardly any airspace congestion, midair collisions had taken place. According to Janes Encyclopeadia of Aviation, the first recorded air collision took place on 8th September 1910 between two aircraft flown by two brothers named Worchacovski in Austria. Another midair collision took place on 2nd October in the same year (1910) when British

Aviation Captain Betram Dickson collided in midair with aircraft flown by French pilot Rens Thomas flying in his Antoinette monoplane. Captain Dickson was injured.

The first midair collision involving commercial aeroplanes appear to have taken place in France on 22nd April 1922 between a Daimler Airways DH 18 flying from London to Paris and a Farman Goliath of the French Airlines Grands Express Aeriens flying from Paris to London. The collision took place about sixty miles north of Paris, while the aircraft were flying through a valley, killing all seven persons on board.

A contemporary newsitem states "The disaster will intensify calls for tighter control of air traffic. At the moment pilots are left a free hand in finding routes and many follow the same ones". Accordingly in December of 1922 'oneway system of routes between London and Paris was set up.

Since then a number of midair collisions have taken place. Listed below are a few of these collisions involving commercial airlines that had taken place during the last forty years.

30th June 1956—Arizona, U.S.A.

A TWA Superconstellation collided with an United Airlines DC-7 over the Grand Canyon in Arizona U.S.A. killing a total of 128 people on board.

16 December 1961—New York, U.S.A.

An United Airlines DC 8 holding to land at New York International Airport (known as Idlewild Airport in those days but now called JFK Airport) collided over the harbour with a TWA Lockheed Superconstellation which was to land at La Guardia Airport. La Guardia Airport is about 4 miles from New York International Airport. A total of 127 passengers and crew were killed. Another 5 people on the ground were also killed due to the scattering of the wreckage over Staten Island and Brooklyn. The lone survivor was a eleven year old boy who was hurled from the tail section of the United Airlines aircraft.

27 March 1977—Tenerife, Canary Islands

A KLM Boeing 747 taking off at Las Rodios Airport in the Canary Islands collided with a Pan American Boeing 747 which was taxiing on the runway. Out of 637 passengers and crew aboard the two aircraft, 575 were killed including everyone on the KLM 747. Actually both aircraft were destined for Las Palmas Airport on the neighbouring island of Gran Canaria, but had been diverted to Las Rodios. They were preparing to make the short hop to Las Palmas and around 5.40 P.M. both had taxied out for take off to the main runway. Only one controller in the tower, at that time could speak English and that too in 'heavily accented English'. To add to that problem there was thick fog at that time. The KLM Boeing 747 started its take off roll when the Pan American aircraft was still on the runway and the 350 ton aircraft hurtled down straight into the Pan American aircraft.

A similar accident almost occurred at Mumbai Airport during April 92 when an Air India Airbus had taken off from the main runway when an Indian Airlines airbus was also on that runway. The Indian Airlines aircraft which had landed earlier was instructed to backtrack that is completely reverse and taxi down the runway as the taxitrack at the end of the runway through which the aircraft would normally have made its exit from the runway was closed. The Air India Airbus was cleared to line up and hold on the runway. The aircraft however took off even before obtaining the actual take off clearance. It got airborne and flew over the Indian Airlines aircraft which was almost at the far end of the runway. A collision was fortuitously averted.

11th August 1979—Ukraine C.I.S.

Two Aeroflot TU 134s collided near Dneprodzerzinsk in Ukraine, killing 165 people.

The next midair collision involving commercial aircraft was the one that took place over Charkhi Dadri on the evening of 12th November 1996.

In India, to the best of my knowledge 3* midair collisions have taken place. The earliest one took place sometime around 1955 over Bombay in which a flying club aircraft flown by a priest was involved. The second one took place about 15 years ago between two training aircraft in Patiala leaving no survivors. The third one was the midair collision between Saudi Arabian Airlines Boeing 747 and Air Kazakhstan Ilyushin 11 76 about 3 km from Charkhi Dadri in the Bhiwani district of Haryana on the evening of 12th November 1996.

The circumstances under which the collision occurred are as follows. Saudi Arabian Airlines Boeing 747 operating flight number SV 763 had taken off from Delhi Airport at 6:33 P.M. on 12th November 96 bound for Dharan in the Middle-east. It had 312 persons on board including 23 crew. Air Kazakhstan Ilyushin IL 76 operating freight charter flight number KZA 1907 had taken off from Chimkent in Kazakhstan and was bound for Delhi Airport. Its estimated time of arrival (ETA) Delhi was 6:45 P.M. It had 37 persons on board. Both aircraft were flying on the same route Golf 452 in opposite directions.

At busy airports, whereever possible, separate routes for departures and arrivals are prescribed for expeditious channeling of air traffic. But at Delhi due airspace restrictions, the same route was used for arrivals and departures in the Western sector. The airspace restrictions stem from military requirement of airspace for various purposes. In Delhi flight information region. 70% of the area is under restricted airspaces while the average figure for India as a whole (land area only) is about 35%.

Wherever a single route is specified for arrivals and departures, one of the methods adopted by the air traffic control to separate incoming and outgoing aircraft is as follows; The incoming aircraft is descended to an appropriate level and the outgoing aircraft is allowed to climb to a level 1000 feet below. As soon as it is established either by means of distances reported from the DME (distance measuring equipment) or by the use of radar that the aircraft have crossed each other, the incoming aircraft

* According to a news item there was a mid-air collision between two IAF MIG aircraft on 22 June 97 landing at Chhabua airbase in Assam in which two pilots died.

is given further descent and the outgoing further climb. At the outset it is not possible for the controller to determine exactly the intermediate levels for climb and descent that would be most appropriate. The descent and climb are therefore given in steps.

This was the procedure followed by ATC Delhi for separating SV 763 and KZA 1907. The approach (radar) controller cleared the Saudi aircraft to climb to FL 140 (14,000 feet) and cleared the Kazakh aircraft to descend to FL 150 (15,000 feet).

At about 6:39 P.M. Saudi reported approaching FL 140 and was asked to maintain the level. Immediately after the Kazakh aircraft reported reaching FL 150. At that time as per the radar controller's message to KZA 1907 the two aircraft were 14 miles apart. They should have crossed in about a minute and a half, separated vertically by the required vertical distance of 1000 feet.

But the aircraft collided with each other. The blips disappeared from the radar screen. An U.S. support aircraft on flight from Islamabad to Delhi bringing supplies to the American Embassy which happened to be flying in that area (on a different route) witnessed the collision. An account of the collision in the words of Captain Timothy J Palace, Commander of the U.S aircraft is given below :

"We were in the clear when a cloud to our two O'clock position lit up. The light was orange in colour and its intensity continued to increase. We were somewhere between 12,000 feet and 14,000 feet. The cloud, from what I saw as it lit up, was about 20-40 miles from us, about 20-30 miles in length in a line about even with or slightly below our altitude. As the cloud lit up I remarked that it must be a rocket launch. The intensity continued to increase and involve the entire cloud. Then a plume of fire came out of the cloud on the right, followed shortly after by one on the left. The direction of movement was hard to determine and we were trying to identify what we were seeing. I remarked that's not a missile, is it? I think this was just prior to or about the same time the second plume appeared. Captain Marks was flying in the right seat and started to bank the aircraft to the left. After a short while (about ten seconds) it became evident that the plumes were descending to the ground. Finally the glow of the cloud diminished, and the two plumes reached the ground continuing to burn as two distinct fires. That's when we realised that it might have been a midair collision. Captain Incerpi was working the radius from the left seat and he informed the controller of what we had just witnessed. The controller made several attempts to contact the two aircraft with no replies."

The spot of the collision was about 3 km from the township of Charkhi Dadri in the district of Bhiwani in Haryana. The wreckage was strewn in a trail 7 km long and 2 km wide, about 40 NM west of Delhi Airport. The black boxes of both the aircraft were recovered from the wreckage. The Saudi 747 lay buried in a crater created by the force of the impact which was about 100 feet long, 20 feet wide and 20 feet deep. All the 349 persons on board the two aircraft lost their lives. Luckily on one on the ground was either killed or injured.

Why did the collision occur when the aircraft were reported to be at different levels separated by 1000 feet?

The Government of India constitued a Court of Inquiry headed by Hon Justice R.C. Lahoti, Judge of the Delhi High Court to investigate the accident. The Court of Inquiry was intially given 3 months to complete the inquiry and its term was extended for a further period of 5 months in two extensions. Submissions were made on behalf of Airports Authority of India, Director General of Civil Aviation, Saudi Airlines, Kazakhstan Government and the Air Traffic Controllers' Guild. The Hon Judge placed his findings before the Government of India in July 97.

The findings of the Court of Inquiry reveal that the root and proximate cause of the collision was the unauthorised descent by the Kazakhstan aircraft to FL 140 instead of maintaining the assigned level of FL 150.

The findings discount sabotage and mechanical failure as possible causes of the accident. The findings also hold that ATC Delhi had acted in accordance with ICAO standards and that the Saudi aircraft had maintained FL 140 strictly in accordance with ATC clearance.

The reasons for the Kazakhstan aircraft to disregard the clearance of ATC Delhi to maintain FL 150 was due to inadequate knowledge of English language on the part of the flying crew.

The scenario in the cockpit during the last minutes of the flight was like this; the Kazakh aircraft had a pilot-in-command, a co-pilot, a flight engineer, a navigator and a radio operator. The radio operator sitting behind the co-pilot was the person who was communicating with ATC Delhi and conveying the clearances to the flying crew. At 6:39 P.M. when the Radio Operator reported reaching FL 150, the aircraft was actually at about 16,500 feet in a descending mode. At that time the aircraft was 14 miles away from the Saudi aircraft. The Kazakh aircraft continued descent through FL 150 and was at FL 140, 25 seconds before the collision. There were some exchanges between the pilots and the Radio Operator regarding the level assigned by ATC Delhi. A few seconds before the collision the Radio Operator cried out "Go to 150 because on the 140 uh that one uh.....!"

The purpose of an inquiry is not primarily to attribute blame but to ensure appropriate preventive measures for the future. Accordingly the Hon Court has made certain recommendations. Among them are that proficiency in the use of the English language on the part of the flying crew should be ensured, that the bi-directional route Golf 452 should be bifurcated into separate departure and arrival routes and that public transport aircraft should be equipped with ACAS (Airborne Collision Avoidance System). The Airports Authority of India has already taken action to bifurcate route Golf 452 and the Director General of Civil Aviation, India has made it mandatory for aeroplanes having a passenger seating configuration of more than 30 or a maximum payload capacity of 3 tonnes to be equipped with ACAS from and after 1st January 1999.

The report also contains recommendations regarding the profession of air traffic control. The report notes that in the organisational set-up of the Airports Authority of India the highest post which an ATC professional can fill is that of Executive Director and considers it inadequate. It specifically recommends that the Airports Authority of India should have a Member (ATC) on the board to look after ATC matters.

6

Black Box—A Brief Description

The term 'Black Box' on an aircraft refers to two equipment namely Cockpit Voice Recorder (CVR) and Flight Data Recorder (FDR). The colour of this box is actually 'fire orange'. The term 'black box' is probably used due to the fact that the contents of the boxes are blocked out—not known to anyone till they are decoded.

The Cockpit Voice Recorder (CVR) is nothing but an ordinary tape recorder capable of recording four channels. Channel 3 normally records pilot's voice, channel 2 th co-pilot's voice, channel 1 the flight engineer's voice and channel 4 the microphone. The CVR is required to record aural environment in the cockpit. Hence it records all warnings generated by different computers. The traps is enclosed in a thermally insulated catridge. Hence the tape will not get affected even if the CVR happens to be inside the burning aircraft. The CVR is normally located in the tailcone of fixed wing aeroplanes, as this is the safest location in the case of an accident. The tape is an endless tape, capable of recording voices/sound upto 30 minutes. The earlier recorded information is erased and new information is recorded on the same tape. The CVR is required to function throughout the flight.

The Digital Flight Data Recorder (DFDR) records the essential parameters of the flight namely heading, airspeed, altitude and vertical speed with reference to time frame. The older versions were capable of recording only five parameters. The modern

DFDRs are capable of recording even upto 200 parameters like position of control surfaces, roll/pitch angle, localizer deviation, glide slope deviation, auto pilot status, all engine parameters like rotor speeds, oil pressure, fuel flow etc. The entire flight envelope can be reconstructed with the help of the DFDR readout. Normally this unit is also located along with the CVR. The information stored in the DEDR has to be decoded with the help of a computer.

Both the CVR and the DFDR carry an 'underwater acoustic beacon' installed on the front face. This beacon will get activated if the black box gets immersed in water. The beacon produces acoustic waves which can be detected through a hydrophone worn by a diver. This enables the unit to be retrieved from the water.

7

Indian Air Traffic Services System

India has been assigned the responsibility for provision of air traffic services within a huge volume of airspace comprising not merely the airspace over the physical boundaries of India, but including also a sizable volume of airspace over the Arabian Sea, Bay of Bengal and the Indian Ocean. It covers an area of about 2.8 million square nautical miles which is equal to nearly 10 million square km. This is equal to roughly 1/60th of the area of the earth's surface. This airspace is divided into five 'flight information regions (FIRs) of Delhi, Mumbai, Calcutta, Chennai and Guwahati. (Fig. 7.2). Within these flight information regions are located the control areas within which full responsibility for avoidance of collisions is assumed by air traffic control. Outside the limits of these control areas but within the flight information regions, responsibility of air traffic control is limited to providing advice and information useful for the safe and efficient conduct of flights, including information on 'collision hazards'.

There are at present ten control areas with the area control centres located at Delhi, Mumbai Calcutta, Chennai, Trivandrum, Hyderabad, Ahmedabad, Guwahati, Varanasi and Nagpur. One more control area is planned to be established at Mangalore. (Fig. 7.1)

A large portion of the airspace over India itself lies beyond the boundaries of these nine control areas. Almost of the whole of the airspace over the oceanic areas also, lies outside the limit of these control areas.

Radar service is available only within the airspace around Delhi, Mumbai, Calcutta, Mumbai, Hyderabad, Nagpur and Trivandrum. Installation of radars at Ahmedabad and Guwahati is nearing completion.

India is strategically located between the nations of Southeast Asia and the nations of the Middle-east, Eastern and Central Europe. Aircraft flying between Southeast Asia/Australia and the nations of the Middle-east, Eastern and Central Europe have to cross the Indian airspace. A number of international air-routes traverse the airspace included within the Indian flight information regions. As a result nearly 40% of the air traffic over India and the Indian FIRs comprise international flights.

The air traffic in the next ten years is expected to grow at the rate of 7.2% P.a.* The air traffic services system in India will have to meet the requirements which this increasing volume of traffic will call for. For this it is necessary that the airspace over at least the whole of the Indian territory would have to be upgraded to the status of controlled airspaces with radar coverage. This will increase the capacity of the air traffic services system by allowing separation between aircraft to be considerably reduced and will also contribute towards safer and more efficient control of air traffic.

The revenue for provision of air traffic services is derived by the levy of two types of charges. Landing charges which is levied on each landing an aircraft makes and route navigation flight charges which is a levy on flight of aircraft from one location to another within Indian airspace. At present charges are levied on a slab system based on the weights of the aircraft; With the result that heavier aircraft pay more by way of both landing and route navigation charges. But in respect of route navigation charges the distance flown within Indian airspace is not considered for levy of charges. That is an aircraft will pay the same whether it flies 500km or 2000 km in Indian airspace.

---

*The projected growth in the Asia-Pacific Region was put at 7.5% p.a. earlier. However in the wake of financial and economic turbulence witnessed in this Region, the International Airline Transportation Association (IATA) has scaled down growth rate for passenger traffic to 4.4% p.a.

However in accordance with international practice there is a proposal to levy route navigation flight charges based both on weight as well as the distance flown.

India as pointed out in the beginning, has been assigned responsibility for provision of air traffic services over a huge volume of airspace. This is both a responsibility as well as an opportunity. Aircraft of practically every nationality overfly Indian airspace. An efficient air traffic system will therefore enhance the prestige of India in the eyes of other nations. It will also contribute to Indian revenues in the form of much valued foreign exchange.

India cannot afford to be complacent in regard to providing a high quality of air traffic services in the belief that international aircraft have no choice other than to overfly India in their flights from east to west and vice versa and that it is a purely 'sellers' market'. Already there is a possibility emerging of China's throwing open some overland air routes for international traffic. China appears to be a bit tardy in this regard but when it does open up its skies India is likely to lose about 20% of its international traffic since many nations will opt to fly these routes even if they are slightly longer if they perceive that they will receive distinctly better service. Pakistan is making a determined bid to bring under its control a huge chunk of airspace over the Arabian Sea west of Mumbai, presently under the jurisdiction of ATC Mumbai on the plea that they are in a position to provide better service. This will of course bring more revenue to Pakistan by way of route navigation flight charges and what is Pakistan's gain will be India's loss.

The Airports Authority of India in an effort to improve the air traffic services in India has embarked upon a project for modernisation of the air traffic services at Delhi and Mumbai (MATS BD Project). This project which is nearing completion is expected to enhance significantly, aircraft handling capacity at these two airports. The following chapter gives a brief description of the salient features of the project.

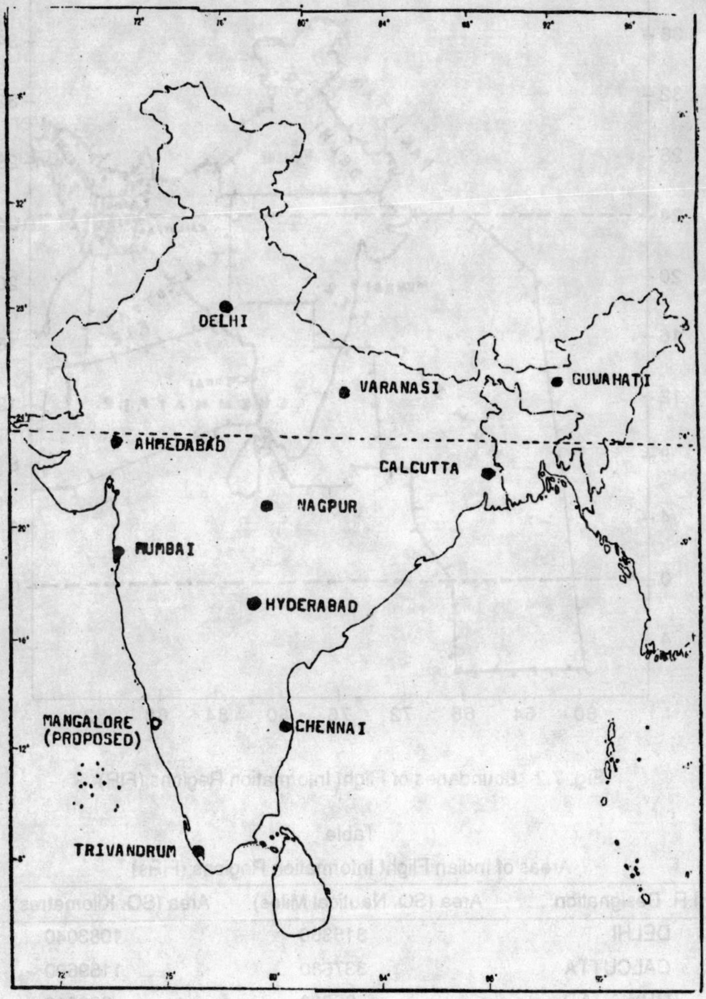

Fig. 7.1 : Locations of Area Control Centres

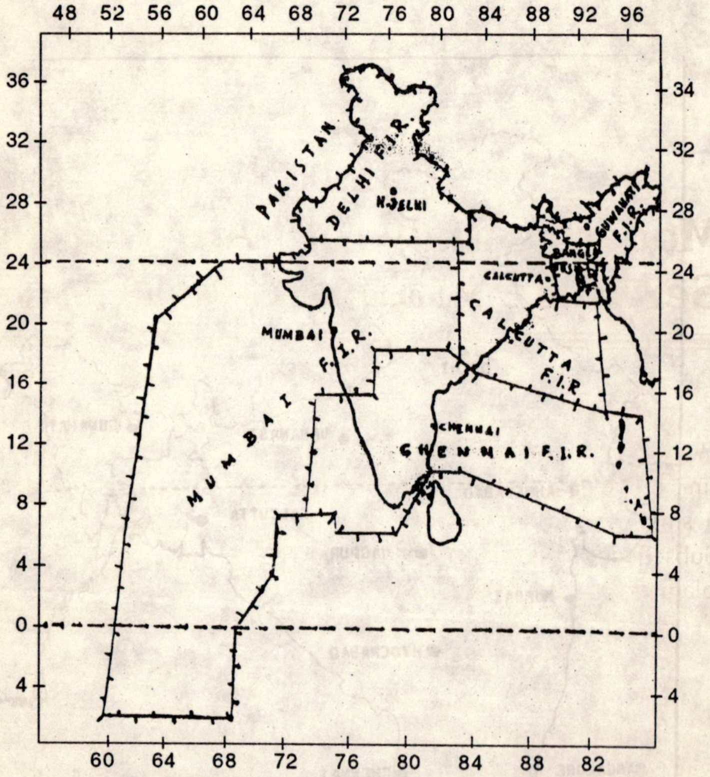

Fig. 7.2 : Boundaries of Flight Information Regions (FIR)

Table

Areas of Indian Flight Information Regions (FIRs)

F.I.R. Designation	Area (SQ. Nautical Miles)	Area (SQ. Kilometres)
DELHI	315360	1083040
CALCUTTA	337680	1159690
GUWAHATI	89280	306610
CHENNAI	663840	2279830
MUMBAI	1399320	4805690
Total	2805480	9634860

Area of India is 3288000 Sq. km; Total area of Indian FIRs is 2.93 times the area of India.

(1 Nautical mile = 1.1515 Statute mile = 1.8532 km.

8

Modernisation of Air Traffic Services : Mumbai-Delhi (Mats BD Project)

The project for modernisation of the air traffic control facilities, equipment and procedures at Mumbai and Delhi was first mooted in the year 1986. At that time it was conceived on a small scale with a proposed outlay of about Rs. 16 crores. Subsequently as the project captured the imagination of the planners its scope and reach were widened till it was finally decided to embark on a programme of full scale modernisation.

Tender specifications running into some four volumes were prepared and global tenders were invited in the year 1993. Three parties responded-Thompson CSF of France, Selenia of Italy and Raytheon Corporation of the U.S.A. The contract was awarded to the Raytheon Corporation of the U.S.A.

The 'System Mission' of the MATS BD project as stated in the Project Information Bulletin is as follows :

"The major activity within this programme is the establishment of automated air traffic control centres at Delhi and Bombay with the objective of achieving enhanced air traffic handling capacity with utmost flight safety. The introduction of automation in air traffic services will reduce delays in landing and take off of aircraft resulting in fuel savings and increase in traffic handling capacity by threefold from the present 12-

15 landings/take offs per hour to 35-40 movements per hour. Additional facilities in the project will greatly reduce the possibilities of diversions of flights thereby minimising inconvenience to passengers and subsequent loss to airlines."

The Airports Authority of India (National Airports Authority at that time) had entered into a contract with Raytheon Corporation of the U.S.A. on a turnkey basis which included supply, installation testing and commissioning of all the navigation and automation equipment. Training was also to be provided to the operational and maintenance personnel by Raytheon. The target date for completion was set at 30 months from date of making the first advance payment i.e 15-10-95. The total cost of the project as envisaged at the time of entering into the contract was Rs. 352 crores (approximately $ 115 million based on exchange rate of that time) which included a foreign exchange component of Rs. 242 crores (approximately $ 80 million).

The target date for completion of the project was therefore 15-10-95, but it could not meet its deadline. Now, more than 2 years after the target date, the project is in the final stages of completion.

The salient features of the project are as follows :

— Construction of entirely new building complexes for control tower and technical block at Mumbai and Delhi.

— Installation of new terminal area radar (TAR) with colocated monopulse secondary surveillance radar (MSSR).

— Installation of air route surveillance radar (ARSR) with colocated monopulse secondary surveillance radar (MSSR).

— Replacement of existing instrument landing systems (ILS) for runway 27 and runway 28 at Delhi and for runway 27 at Mumbai and installation of additional (new) instrument landing systems (ILS) for runway 10 at Delhi and for runways 09 and runway 14 at Mumbai.

— Installation of terminal VORS (TVOR) at four locations around Delhi Airport and three locations around Mumbai Airport and formulation of standard instrument departure procedures (STD) and standard terminal arrival routes (STAR) for Delhi and Mumbai.

— Installation of training simulators at Delhi and Mumbai.

— Auxiliary facilities like flight data processing system (FDPS), radar data processing system (RDPS), voice communication control system (VCCS), automatic self briefing system (ASBS) and system work stations.

Each of the above features is briefly explained below :

Construction of building complexes; This portion of the project was not actually part of the contract awarded to Raytheon but was executed by the Airports Authority of India through indigenous contractors. The construction work commenced at Delhi during May 93 and completed in 1995. It has a floorspace of 14,000 sq m, height of 60 m and cost Rs. 24 crores. The construction work commenced at Mumbai during October 93 and was completed in 1995. It has a floorspace of 14,750 sq m, height of 60 m and projected cost of Rs. 23 crores.

Installation of terminal area radars (TAR); New Terminal area radars with a range of 60 NM (at an altitude of 38,000 feet) have been installed. The TAR is a primary surveillance radar operating in the 'S' band, that is with a wavelength of 10cm. Colocated with the TAR is an monopulse secondary surveillance radar (MSSR) operating in the 'L' band, that is with a wavelength of 30 cm. The monopulse technique provides improved performance as compared to conventional secondary surveillance radar systems.

The system is provided with a situation data display. This is an electronic display in which synthetic tracks of the aircraft flying within the range of the radar will be presented by combining the plots derived from the TAR and colocated MSSR.

Installation of air route surveillance radars (ARSR); New air route surveillance radars with a range of 220 NM (at an altitude of 72,000 feet) have been installed. The ARSR is a primary surveillance radar operating in the 'L' band, that is a wave length of 30 cm. Colocated with the ARSR is a monopulse secondary surveillance radar (MSSR) also operating in the 'L' band. The maximum range of interrogation of the MSSR is 250 NM at 66,000 feet.

Synthetic tracks of the aircraft flying within the range of the ARSR/MSSR will be presented on the situation data display by combining plots derived from the ARSR and colocated MSSR.

Installation of instrument landing systems (ILS);

The existing ILS for runways 27 and 28 at Delhi have been replaced with new equipment and a new ILS has been installed for runway 10. At Mumbai the existing ILS for runway 27 has been replaced and new ILS had been installed for runway 14. An ILS is yet to be installed for runway 09.

Installation of terminal VORs (TVOR); Terminal VORS are VORs of low power and limited range. They are intended to provide navigational guidance in terminal areas i.e to facilitate approach and departures in the areas around busy airports. Four such TVORs have been installed around Delhi.

Standard instrument departures (SID) as well as standard terminal arrival routes (STAR) have been formulated for Delhi and Mumbai, based on the TVORs, STARs are prescribed routings for arriving aircraft to make an approach to the airports depending on the runway-in-use. SIDs are prescribed routings for departing aircraft to join their intended tracks, again depending on the runway in use. These routings have been worked out utilising a computer simulator model called the SIMMOD. This is the first time that such STARs/SIDs will be in application in India.

The STARs/SIDs are intended to facilitate an expeditious and smooth flow of traffic with considerable reduced need for pilot/controller exchanges; each STAR/SID is identified by an appropriate designator and the use of the designator will enable air traffic control to avoid lengthy descriptions of the manoeuvres to be executed by the pilot.

Training Simulator; the modernisation package provided by Raytheon includes a training simulator both for Delhi and for Mumbai. The simulator will enable local training of controllers in a real life scenario. The exercises can be planned in advance and any number of 'aircraft' can be injected into the exercise. The controller can therefore be trained to handle traffic in excess of what he may normally encounter.

Flight data processing system (FDPS); Air traffic control units receive flight plan of aircraft from various aerodromes/ air traffic control units which give concise information regarding flights about to take place. The information contained in the flight plans have to be processed i.e extracted and recast in a suitable and convenient form usually in the form of a flight progress strip to enable the controller to know the details and estimates of the flights about to take place within his area of jurisdiction. This work has so far been performed in India manually, which is time consuming and prone to errors. The FDPS enables the processing to be done automatically on the computer including automatic printing out of the flight progress strips. This technique already in use over many years in other countries is being introduced in India for the first time.

The FDPS incorporates software with two interesting additional features; one, a traffic conflict alert (TCA) to warn the controller in advance of potential traffic conflicts and two, a visual display which presents the controller with a synthetic track data of all aircraft within the FIR.

Radar data processing system (RDPS); The radar data processing system (RDPS) is a computer software which processes the signals received at the radar heads (i.e antenna) of the primary and secondary surveillance radars from the aircraft flying within the range of the radars. This processed output is presented on the controllers' display. Multi-radar tracking (MRT) has the capability to combine data for a target (i.e an aircraft) from several radar heads to provide a single track, that is, symbol on the controllers' display. This gives continuity of track when any one radar does not detect the target for some reason or the other. The RDPS has also the capability to interact with the FDPS to update flight plan information.

Voice communication control system (VCCS); This is an equipment to provide access to the controller to the various radio and telephone facilities required for the purpose of control of air traffic. It integrates all the radio and telephone functions on to a single control panel at the controllers' work station. By just selecting an appropriate switch, the controller is enabled to select any desired communication facility, either radio or telephone.

Automatic self briefing system (ASBS); It is an information system which provides an automatic method of receiving, storing and retrieving data required for pilots' preflight briefing.

It provides current information on the availability and status of aerodrome and ground aids like runways, taxiways and so on, visual aids like the lighting systems, navigation aids like the VOR, ILS, communication facilities as well as information on activities hazardous to air navigation like firing ranges.

System work stations; System work station refers to the complex of various sub systems mounted on a desk which enables the controller seated in front of it to make use of the various facilities available to perform his job. Each air traffic control unit i.e tower, approach control, area control and so on have different types of work stations to meet the requirements of that unit. The system work stations are designed with regard to ergonomic principles, aesthetics as well as promoting correct and comfortable posture for working over lengthy periods.

This, in a nutshell is the MATS BD (Modernisation of Air Traffic Services Bombay Delhi) Project regarding which newsitems appear frequently in the press. This project, planned to be fully completed by 15 October 1995 has already suffered a time overrun of over two years. The project has also exceeded the original played outlay of Rs. 352 crores ($ 115 million) by about Rs. 70 crores ($ 20 million).

The delay in the completion of the project has led to criticism particularly in the context of the mid-air collision over Charkhi Dadri near Delhi on 12 November 96, whence it was pointed out that had the Delhi ARSR/MSSR been commissioned as per schedule, the collision would have been averted as the radar would have indicated that the Kazakh aircraft had descended below its assigned level of flight level 150; which information was not available to the controller in the absence of the facility. The causes for the delay in the commissioning of the project appear to be on account of the following factors :

Firstly, the project involved construction of huge technical complexes at Delhi and Mumbai and while the building at Delhi progressed well there was delay in respect of Mumbai due to problems of water seepage from underground water conduits as well as on account of the severe monsoon of 1993-94. Work of actual installation could only take place after completion of the buildings and delay in the construction of the buildings resulted in delay in the implementation of the project.

Secondly, the project involved import of hitech equipment on a large scale for which customs clearance had to be obtained as well as approval from the Director General of Civil Aviation for claiming rebate in customs duties. All this involved the inevitable procedural delays.

Thirdly, land had to be acquired in small pockets at a number of places for installing the TVORs and so on which was a time consuming process.

Fourthly, the TVORs were located at remote places their locations having been selected to best serve the inbound and outbound routings of aircraft. Some of these locations lacked basic facilities like approach roads, power connection all of which had to be provided. New buildings had to be erected for housing the localizers, radar antenna equipment and so on.

Fifthly the installation of the facilities had to meet the specification of the Airports Authority of India and where they were not considered meeting the specifications, changes had to be made resulting in some delay.

It appears in retrospect that the planned duration of 30 months for the project was unduly optimistic or even unrealistic considering that the project had many facets, a very wide scope and reach and required to be executed in an environment well known for its procedural delays and tangles.

Assuming that the project is completed and does live up to its expectations what would be its impact on the Indian aviation scenario?

The thrust of the MATS BD project, as mentioned in the System Mission is on increasing the traffic handling capacity at Delhi and Mumbai Airports to about 35-40 movements per hour. But even if the air traffic control system at the two airports does achieve the capability to handle 40 movements per hour, in actual practice this is not likely to be realised on account of constraints of other arms of the operational infrastructure, namely the system of taxiways and parking stands. If we assume that the peak traffic comprises 20 departures and 20 arrivals, the departures and arrivals being equally divided between international and domestic operations, then we would expect 10 international departures and arrivals and 10 domestic departures and arrivals per hour. Assume also that the parking stand occupancy time for international aircraft is 2 hours and for domestic aircraft 1 hour. We further assume that all the aircraft at the airport are visiting aircraft only, that is no aircraft is based at that airport to occupy the parking stands for prolonged periods. Then it is easy to see that this would lead to a requirement of a minimum of 30 parking stands at each of the two airports. In actual practice the requirement would be much higher as some aircraft are in actuality based at Delhi and Mumbai and all the stands do not permit independent entry and exit in and out of the stand which is implicitly assumed in the illustration. Another assumption in the illustration is that there are no constraints with respect to aircraft type for accommodating aircraft in the parking stands which assumption is also very unrealistic.

The enhanced volume of traffic must also be matched by enhanced passenger handling facilities. Considering only international movements, 10 arrivals and 10 departures per hour means that an aircraft would be coming into the stand every 6 minutes and leaving the stand every 6 minutes. Even conservatively taking the average number of passengers per aircraft as 200, it means an inflow of 2000 passengers per hour and outflow of the same number. It appears highly unlikely that the passenger handling facilities including customs etc would be able to deal with such a high rate of inflow and outflow.

As on today it is also doubtful if either of the two airports can accommodate 30 aircraft at a time. Even under the existing conditions paucity of parking space has been one other main constraints in accepting more aircraft at Delhi and Mumbai.

Again if we look at the salient features of the MATS BD project we would note that it makes no mention of air-ground communication facilities except for the VCCS which is just a panel for accessing the communication channels. The intention is to attend to the communication requirements departmentally and efforts are being made to improve the communication system to match the requirements of the enhanced scale of operations. However poor communications has been the persistent bane of air traffic control and there appears to be little reason to believe that the situation would improve in the future. Without good communications there can be no good air traffic control.

Lastly, the MATS BD project concerns itself only with the modernisation of facilities at two pockets of Delhi and Mumbai. The Indian Air Traffic System is however a huge one and as mentioned earlier it comprises an area of about 2.8 million sq NM. The system as a whole must be able to sustain and feed the planned peak traffic at Delhi and Mumbai. For this there should be continous areas of radar coverage and reliable communication over a much wider area. No doubt plans are afoot to modernise Calcutta and Chennai and MSSRs have been installed or under installation at Trivandrum, Guwahati, Hyderabad and Ahmedabad. But isolated areas of radar coverage do not help except for limited use for separation of traffic.

9

Air Navigation System for Future

The system of air traffic control described in the previous chapters had evolved over the years, gradually increasing in degree of sophistication in technology to meet matching requirements of increase in sophistication of aircraft design, as well as increase in the volume of air traffic. Yet with the steady increase in aircraft movements throughout the sixties, seventies and the eighties, there was bound to be a stage where the existing systems capacity would come to be stretched at many points and saturated at some. Realising this, the International Civil Aviation Organisation responded in the early eighties by establishing a special committee on Future Air Navigation Systems (the FANS Committee). The Committee was charged with studying, identifying and assessing new concepts and new technology including satellites and to make recommendations for the coordinated evolutionary development of air navigation into the 21st century. It was to be a global systems approach.

Thus began the long range planning process aimed at utilising the potential of satellites for air navigation, that is for facilitating air navigation as well as air traffic control.

The FANS Committee brought to this vital task a remarkable depth of resources in talent and expertise. It took just about four years to complete this mammoth task.

Originally termed as Future Air Navigation Systems (FANS) the new system was renamed as the ICAO CNS ATM System-

C, N, and S standing for communications, navigation and surveillance and ATM standing for air traffic management.

The process of getting an aircraft safely and efficiently to its destination has been classified by the ICAO into three functions—communications, navigation and surveillance.

Communications is the exchange of information through 'voice' and or 'data' between aircraft and air traffic control. 'Voice' refers to exchange through 'aural' means, that is actual speech while 'data' refers to exchanges through visual means, that is alphanumeric displays. Navigation is the process of determining the position of an aircraft for the aircrew. Surveillance is the process of making available to air traffic control, positions and changes in positions of aircraft from time to time; air traffic control may obtain these positions by means of pilots' reports or by some other means independent of the pilot.

ATM or air traffic management is a broadly defined function which includes air traffic control, air traffic flow management, that is, ensuring an optimum flow of air traffic at times when air traffic congestion exceeding capacity of the air traffic system is anticipated and lastly air space management, that is, maximising the utilization of available airspace within a given air space structure. Based on these concepts the new futuristic system was rechristened as the ICAO CNS ATM system. The report of the FANS committee was submitted to an ICAO world wide Air Navigation Conference in September 1991 and was unequivocally endorsed. India was also a participant in the conference. During December 1991 the ICAO CNS ATM system was approved by ICAO.

The elements of the ICAO CNS ATM System is briefly described in relation to the existing system.

Communications

In the existing system [Fig. 9.1 (a)] communications between aircraft and air traffic control is mainly through 'voice' using frequencies in the very high frequency (VHF) range (118 to 136 MHz) in terminal areas that is in areas of heavy traffic and using high frequency (HF) in other areas including oceanic airspaces. VHF communications are generally free of distortion and static but the range is limited on account of the constraint of its property of 'line of sight' transmission. Generally the range of a VHF transmitter will be equal to 4/3 $\sqrt{A}$ in *nautical miles* where A is the height of the aircraft in *feet* that is if an aircraft is at a height of 10,000 feet it can be heard for a maximum distance of about 4/3 × $\sqrt{10000}$ = 130 nautical miles. Beyond that distance at that height it will not be able to communicate with the air traffic control. [Fig. 8.1 (c)] HF transmissions are not subject to this constraint as the waves can 'bend' but they suffer from shortcomings like severe fading, interference and static and are not reliable.

In the future system, [Fig. 9.1 (b)] communications between aircraft and the air traffic control would be through VHF voice and data and in addition through SSR Mode S data in terminal areas (areas of generally high density of traffic) and through AMSS voice and data in other areas. 'VHF voice' is the same as in the present environment while 'VHF Data' refers to exchanges through visual means that is alphanumeric displays. The advantage of data communications over voice communications is that it involves less physical strain and is less prone to errors caused by misunderstanding. 'SSR Mode S Data' is data communications through radar interface. The 'S' stands for 'selective link' that is, facility of selectively addressing a particular aircraft for transmission of information. A radar associated with this facility enables information to be passed to an aircraft which is displayed on the radar console. The scope of this method for exchanges of messages between air traffic control and aircraft is limited.

'AMSS Voice/Data' refers to satellited based system of exchanges through voice or through data communications. AMSS stands for 'Aeronautical Mobile Satellite Service' which is defined as a system of airground communications via satellites using frequency band allocated for aeronautical purposes. This is mainly for use in areas other than terminal areas (where the volume of traffic will be comparatively less) and over vast oceanic airspaces where VHF voice/Data and SSR Mode S are not practicable. Such system of satellite based communications will replace the existing HF communications, and will be free from the shortcomings of the existing system like fading, interference, static and unreliability.

Fig. 9.1 : Communication

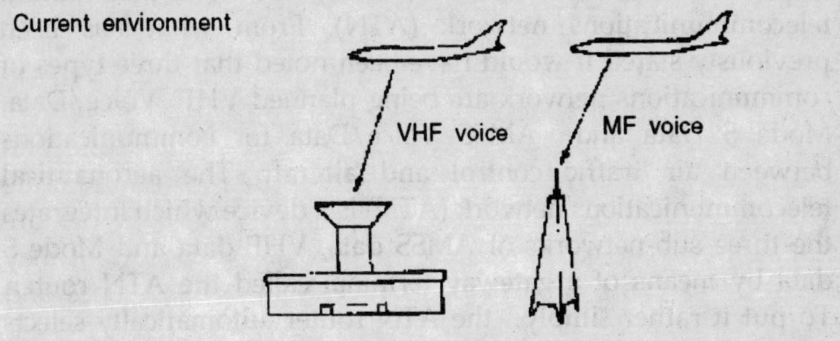

Fig. 9.1 (a)

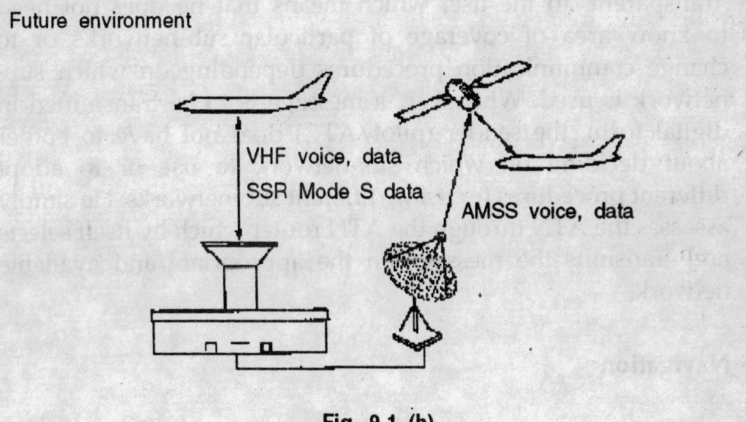

Fig. 9.1 (b)

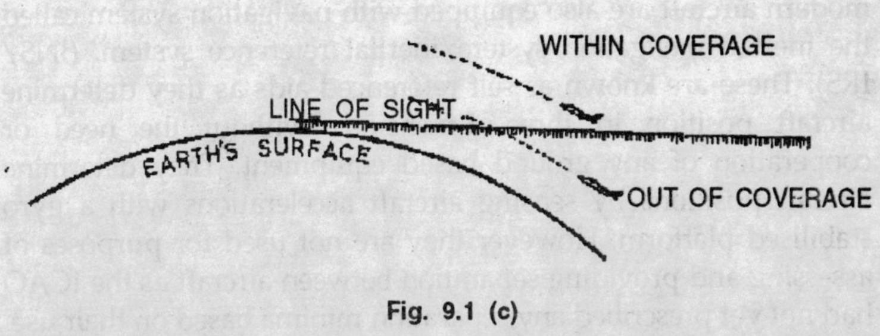

Fig. 9.1 (c)

Another important component of the future system in respect of communications is a facility known as aeronautical telecommunications network (ATN). From what has been previously stated it would have been noted that three types of communications network are being planned VHF Voice/Data. Mode S Data and AMSS Voice/Data for communications between air traffic control and aircraft. The aeronautical telecommunications network (ATN) is a device which integrates the three sub-networks of AMSS data, VHF data and Mode S data by means of a gateway terminal called the ATN router. To put it rather simply, the ATN router automatically selects the appropriate sub-network (VHF data, AMSS data or Mode S data) based on the communications requirement of the user (pilot/ATC) and sub-network availability. This action is 'transparent' to the user which means that he does not need to know area of coverage of particular sub-networks or to change communication procedures depending on which sub-network is used. Whenever a message is to be transmitted in digital form, the sender (pilot/ATC) does not have to bother about deciding on which sub-network to use or to adopt different procedures for using different sub-networks. He simply assesses the ATN through the ATN router which by itself selects and transmits the message on the appropriate and available network.

Navigation

In the existing system [Fig 9.2 (a)] radio navigation aids like the NDB, VOR DME as well as OMEGA are used for navigation. The range of these facilities is limited and these facilities are also prone to frequent failures. These are ground based systems. Many modern aircraft are also equipped with navigation system called the inertial navigation system/inertial reference system. (INS/IRS). These are known as self referenced aids as they determine aircraft position in three dimensions without the need or cooperation of any ground based equipment. They determine aircraft positions by sensing aircraft accelerations with a gyro stabilised platform. However they are not used for purposes of assessing and providing separation between aircraft as the ICAO had not yet prescribed any separation minima based on their use.

In the future system [Fig. 9.2 (b)] the basic approach is to develop a concept of required navigation performance (RNP) which will define the performance required in a particular airspace, or phase of flight. Subject to the condition of such required performance being achieved, any kind of navigation equipment may be used. However the ICAO CNS ATM system is definite in its preference for global navigation satellite system (GNSS) for navigation. This system includes satellite constellations, aircraft receivers and integrity monitoring. It is expected to be the sole means of navigation and will eventually replace the current navigation systems such as NDB, VOR, OMEGA and so on.

GNSS is therefore a satellite based position, time determination system. Two versions of the GNSS are already available, the Global Positioning System (GPS) developed by the Department of Defence of the United States Government and the Global Orbitting Navigation Satellite System (GLONASS) under development by the CIS. A brief system description of the GPS is given below :

The GPS system has the capability to provide geodetic position and velocity in three dimensions plus time. It comprises 24 satellites (21 working and 3 spare) in 12 hour circular orbits in 6 orbital planes the radius of the orbits being 26,000 km. A GPS user determines his position by processing information relating to range, that is distance measurement, of a minimum number of 4 satellites. The satellites continually transmit signals on appropriate frequencies and the range (distance) of the satellite from the user is found by accurately measuring the time taken by signals transmitted by the satellite to reach the aircraft (user in general).

To explain further, if the distance of the aircraft from one such satellite 'P' is known, say 'X' then it is clear that the aircraft lies on a sphere of radius 'X' with centre at 'P' . If a second distance measurement from another satellite 'Q' is made say 'Y' then obviously the aircraft's position is on a circle formed by the intersections of two spheres of radii X and Y, with centres at 'P' and 'Q'. A third distance measurement from satellite 'R' say 'Z' would narrow the probable position to just two points. Since the approximate position of the aircraft is known it is easy

Fig. 9.2 : Navigation

(a) Current environment

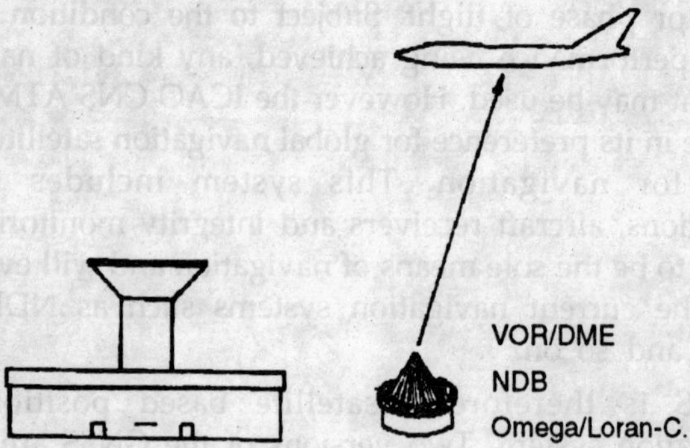

Fig. 9.2 (a)

(b) Future environment

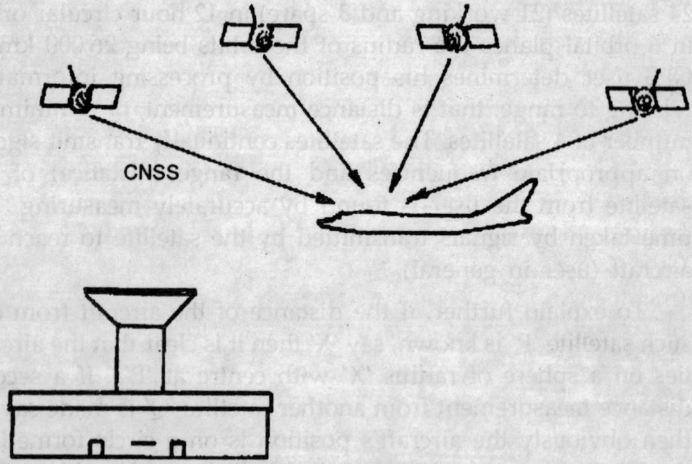

Fig. 9.2 (b)

to eliminate one of the two such possibilities. The positions of the satellites themselves are accurately known and updated periodically. These positions are transmitted continually by the satellite. Thus the aircraft position is determined in the GPS system. Theoretically three range measurements from three satellites are sufficient to determine the position but one problem exists. The distance measurement based on the time taken by the signals emitted by the satellites to reach the aircraft will be correct only if the user (aircraft) clock is correctly synchronized with the satellite clocks. There may be an error in such synchronization and therefore a range measurement from a fourth satellite becomes necessary.

The satellite transmissions are modulated by two codes, a coarse code (CA) and a precision code (P Code). These codes are changed from time to time. Knowledge of these codes is required to access the system.

GPS provides both a standard positioning service (SPS) and a precision positioning service (PPS). SPS will be provided to any user, civil, commercial or others, internationally. It has a level of accuracy set at 100 meters horizontal and 157 metres vertical at 95% probability. The PPS is a military position navigation service providing accuracy higher than SPS but provided only to limited users through requirement of knowledge of the current precision code.

As mentioned already, the ICAO envisages usage of GPS (or GLOSSNAS) as an immediate GNSS system for the CNS/ ATM. These systems are under the full control of two individual nations ICAO expects that an integrated GNSS System would be implemented as an evolutionary progression from existing GPS & GLOSSNAS systems over which contracting states (members of the ICAO) would be able to exercise sufficient level of control on aspects related to its use for civil aviation.

Surveillance

Surveillance as already mentioned earlier is the process of making available to the air traffic control the positions and changes of positions of aircraft. In the existing system [Fig. 9.3 (a)] where radar is not available surveillance is based on position reports made by the aircraft themselves. Aircraft are required to report positions periodically and additional position reports may also be called for by the air traffic control. The position reports provide information on aircraft position, altitude, estimates of future position and optionally on operational (endurance etc) and meteorological information (upper winds, temperature etc.). Within airspace where radar is available, the air traffic control obtain precise information on its own. Primary radar provides information only on geographical position while secondary radar (SSR) provides information on aircraft altitude also. However since range of radar is limited by the properties of line of sight transmission, it cannot be employed over distance oceanic areas.

In the future system [Fig. 9.3 (b)] while retaining the secondary surveillance radar augmented by Mode S for use in areas of high traffic density, a new concept called automatic dependent surveillance (ADS) will be introduced. ADS is a concept whereby information regarding aircraft identification, position, altitude and time can be passed automatically through an air ground data link to the appropriate air traffic control unit. This information is extracted from the aircraft navigation system without the involvement or even awareness of the aircrew. Apart from mere position, altitude and time other information like outside temperature, windspeed and direction at the aircraft's current location may also be tapped. The frequency of the passage of the information may be determined by a 'contract' set up between ground and airborne equipment. This contract may be based on time intervals for example every ten or fifteen minutes or may be based on 'event' for example, passing a particular way point (a specified location at which position reports is required to be made) or passing a particular flight level. Individual contracts are set up with each flight although there can also be 'standard contracts'. Additionally the air traffic control can call for position and other information as and when required. The system has also an emergency capability which can be flight deck triggered.

In other words the 'ADS' enables the controller to 'read' the aircraft instruments! A novel and innovative concept indeed.

I have briefly outlined in the above pages the main features of the ICAO CNS ATM system as compared with the existing

Fig. 9.3 : Surveillance

(a) Current environment

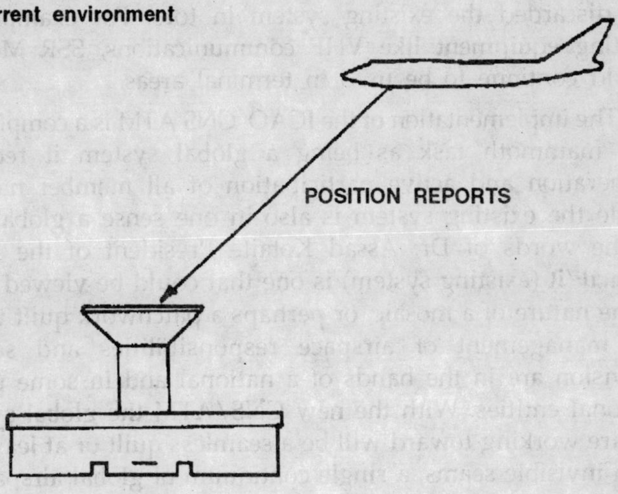

Fig. 9.3 (a)

(b) Future environment

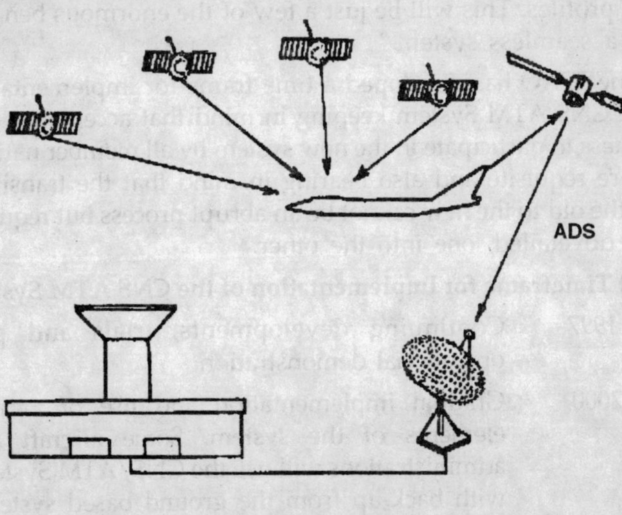

Fig. 9.3 (b)

system. (Summarised in Table 9.1 CNS system Evolution) It may be noted that the FANS committee had, while making innovations not discarded the existing system in toto. For example the existing equipment like VHF communications, SSR Mode S would continue to be used in terminal areas.

The implementation of the ICAO CNS ATM is a complicated and mammoth task as being a global system it requires cooperation and active participation of all member nations. While the existing system is also in one sense a global one, in the words of Dr. Assad Kotaite President of the ICAO council 'it (existing system) is one that could be viewed more in the nature of a mosaic, or perhaps a patchwork quilt where the management of airspace responsibilities and service provision are in the hands of a national and in some places regional entities. With the new CNS/ATM the global system we are working toward will be a seamless quilt or at least one with invisible seams, a single continuum of global airspace. It may be less colourful than the patchwork version of the airspace quilt but for the airline and its customers it will offer a far more practical, flexible safe and efficient operating environment. The technology of today, computers, satellites, data links and advance avionics will eliminate much potential for misunderstanding and allow user preferred routes and flight profiles. This will be just a few of the enormous benefits from a seamless system."

The ICAO has developed a time frame for implementation of the CNS ATM System keeping in mind that acceptance and readiness to participate in the new system by all member nations is a pre requisite and also bearing in mind that the transition from the old to the new cannot be an abrupt process but requires to be dovetailed, one into the other.

ICAO Timeframe for Implementation of the CNS ATM System

Upto 1997 : Continuing developments, trials and pre-operational demonstration.

upto 2000 : Gradual implementation and use of various elements of the system. Some aircraft and administrations will use the CNS/ATM Systems with back-up from the ground based systems.

Table 9.1 : CNS Systems Evolution

Airspace	*Function*	*Current system*	*Future system*
Oceanic Continental enroute airspace with low-density traffic (Note 6)	Navigation	OMEGA/LORAN-C NDB VOR/DME Barometric altimetry INS/!RS	RNAV/RNP GNSS Barometric altimetry GNSS altitude INS/IRS
	Communications *	VHF voice HF voice	VHF voice/data AMSS data/voice HF voice; North and South poles only (Note 5)
	Surveillance	Primary radar/SSR voice position reports	ADS
Continental airspace with high-density traffic	Navigation	OMEGA/LORAN-C NDB VOR/DME Barometric altimetry INS/IRS	RNAV/RNP GNSS Barometric altimetry GNSS altitude (Note 2) INS/IRS
	Communications*	VHF Voice	VHF voice/data AMSS data/voice SSR Mode S data link
	Surveillance	Primary radar SSR Mode A/C	SSR (Mode A/C or Mode S) ADS
Oceanic airspace with high-density traffic	Navigation	MNPS OMEGA/LORAN-C Barometric altimetry INS/IRS	RNAV/RNP GNSS Barometric altimetry GNSS altitude (Note 2) INS/IRS
	Communications*	HF voice	AMSS data/voice
	Surveillance	Voice position reports	ADS
Terminal areas with high density traffic	Navigation	NDB VOR/DME ILS	RNAV/RNP GNSS MLS

Contd...

Airspace	*Function*	*Current system*	*Future system*
		Barometric altimetry INS/IRS	NDB (Note 3) VOR/DME (Note 4) Barometric altimetry INS/IRS
	Communications*	VHF	VHF voice/data SSR Mode S data link AMSS data/voice (Note 7)
	Surveillance	Primary radar SSR Mode A/C	SSR (Mode A/C or Mode S) ADS (Note 1)

Note 1 — The need for primary radar is reduced

Note 2 — To be used where barometric altimetry is not functional, especially at high altitudes

Note 3 — NDB will be progressively withdrawn

Note 4 — VOR/DME will be progressively withdrawn

Note 5 — Until such time as satellite communications are available

Note 6 — Includes low altitude, off shore, and remote areas

Note 7 — Depends on outcome of feasibility studies

* The aeronautical telecommunication network (ATN) based on the International Organization for Standardization (ISO) open system interconnection (OSI) reference model provides for internetworking of aeronautical air ground and ground-ground data links and is applicable to all airspace in future systems.

Source : Global Co-ordinated Plan for the Transition to the ICAO CNS/ATM System.

2000-2005 : Full CNS/ATM services available in parallel with existing systems so that appropriately equipped aircraft could have maximum operating benefits from the CNS/ATM Systems.

2005-2010 : The international ground based systems not required for the CNS/ATM systems progressively dismantled.

2010 : The CNS/ATM Systems are the sole system for international use.

The question now arises as to the advantages and disadvantages of the ICAO CNS ATM System.

Advantages

It is expected that air traffic will grow at a high rate in the years to come, the anticipated growth gate being the highest in the Asia Pacific Region (which includes India) at 7.5 p.a. The existing ground based systems would not be able to handle this volume of traffic. The new CNS ATM System by fully utilising computers, satellites, data links and advanced avionics would provide the required higher capacity for handling of the enhanced volume of air traffic.

As regards the cost aspect, the ICAO has worked out cost benefit analysis and concluded that the new system provides positive net present value (that if it is an acceptable investment). An exercise was also carried out in India in 1994 to assess the cost and benefits of the system under the aegis of the ICAO in which representatives of some other nations like Pakistan, Nepal, Maldives participated (I was a participant on behalf of the Airports Authority of India) and the analysis also indicated positive NPV. However this is not to be taken as conclusive as the analysis was very superficial and the meeting was mainly intended to educate the participants regarding the manner in which the project appraisal should be carried out.

A third reason given in favour of the CNS ATM is that it will increase safety and expedite air traffic. Being a global system based on the use of satellite based aids it will vastly reduce the number of air traffic control units. Many small area control units will be combined to form a larger area control centre. It will also eliminate much potential for misunderstanding and result in saving of fuel and time for individual flights by allowing user preferred routes and flight paths.

Higher capacity, positive NPV, higher safety and traffic expedition; Then what could be the disadvantages?

Some nations have reservations about the advisability of implementing the ICAO CNS ATM System stemming mainly from two factors.

— With the increased involvement of satellite service providers, will the authority and responsibility of individual states over their territory be retained?

That some states, particularly small states apprehend that by globalising an traffic control their authority and responsibility for control of air navigation will go out of their hands. For, if the air traffic services over the entire airspace of a small country is provided by an air traffic control unit of another country because of the process of establishing larger area control centres it is feared that not only their authority may be undermined, the security of their nation may also be compromised. ICAO has, however, assured that 'states authority will be preserved in the coordination and control of communications and in the augmentation as necessary of satellite navigation services.

The second cause of apprehension is the proposed use of GPS/GLOSSNAS for navigation till such time as an integrated GNSS system is established over which contracting states will exercise sufficient level of control on aspects relating to their use. As pointed out earlier, the GPS and GLOSSNAS are under control of the United States of America and the CIS. In the case of GPS as mentioned earlier, knowledge of a certain code (coarse code) is required to access the system. These codes can and are changed from time to time. As a result the use of the system may be denied to any one at the option of the USA. This places the other nations in a vulnerable postion.

In my talks with a few senior level managers of the air traffic administrations of some countries, I could see that this was an aspect to which they were very adversely inclined. But as far as India is concerned, this aspect does not appear to have bothered the policy makers. In India there is enthusiastic support for the ICAO CNS ATM System.

I shall conclude this Chapter by describing the reaction of pilots and controllers to the adoption of the new system. This account is based on the articles in the ICAO Journal of December 1991 by the International Federation of Airlines Pilots Association (IFALPA), London (pp 18-19) and the International Federation of Air Traffic Controllers' Association, London (pp 20-21).

The International Federation of Airline Pilots' Association (IFALPA) has generally welcomed the ICAO CNS ATM System. It sees the future air navigation system concept as the latest and finally successful endeavour to define workable schemes. While admitting that 'space' systems are expensive, the IFALPA lists the advantages accruing from the new system. Increase in system capacity and coverage, increase in air traffic consequent upon more efficient use of air space, significant time and fuel savings to airlines and consequent cost reduction, availability of air traffic services to all areas and regions of the world unconstrained by distance limitations as in the existing ground based systems and savings in size and weight of avionics equipment carried by aircraft.

As regards air traffic controllers, the International Federation of Air Traffic Controllers Association (IFATCA) agrees that the benefits to be derived from the CNS ATM concept will be welcomed by both flight crews and air traffic controllers. It also agrees that the enhanced navigation capability that will be available on a global basis would significantly enhance flight safety and efficiency and capacity.

The International Federation of Air Traffic Controllers Association (IFATCA) has, however, drawn attention to the concerns expressed at times in reducing aircrews to the role of passive monitors rather than active fliers as consequence of automation of flight deck controls. IFATCA apprehends that air traffic controllers may likewise become reliant on automated systems so that active participation is reduced to monitoring status. They have quoted David Hopkins of the Royal Air Force Institute of Aviation Medicine on ATC automation. 'Tasks may become dull, boring and unsatisfactory and ultimately unaccepatable as the opportunities to develop and exercise skills or to become fully and actively involved in the control of air traffic are curtailed.

IFATCA accepts that automation must assist and support air traffic control in the execution of this task but has also drawn attention to the requirement of the new automated system being totally failsafe; if not the controllers will not trust the new system and will be uncomfortable in working.

IFATCA urges that the controller should be retained as the primary decision maker and must continue to be vested with the overall control function in the future ATS Systems. IFATCA also wants the legal implications of automated ATC systems to be ciearly defined and responsibilities determined particularly "where it can be demonstrated that the system caused the accident."

10

Controller and His Job

Who are the types of persons who become air traffic controllers? Considering that this is a highly specialized profession and one regarding which there is very little public awareness, it might be expected that the majority of those entering this profession are those with some kind of prior links by way of having relations working as controllers or in some other capacity at an airport or those who had acquired some qualification relating to aviation. Actually controllers with such kind of background form only a very small proportion. The majority of the controllers are job seekers who have adopted the profession as a means of livelihood.

The basic qualification for recruitment of a controller in the earlier days was graduation in Physics or Mathematics or a degree in Engineering. In the 70s when the job market was poor for engineering graduates many with such qualifications were inducted as controllers. In the middle seventies many pilot licence holders who were unable to get jobs as pilots were taken in as air traffic controllers and the requirement of being a graduate was relaxed in their case. At present the basic qualifications prescribed are a post graduate degree in Science Physics) or an engineering degree. The population of controllers in India, is therefore a mixed bag comprising graduates and post graduates, engineering degree holders and pilot licence holders.

The actual selection of controllers is through a two-stage process. First a written test is held and those that secure a minimum cut off percentage are asked to appear for a viva voce. During the viva voce a 'voice' test is held to make sure that the candidate's voice is suitable and he has no speech impediments. A psychologist also sits on the interview board. Considering the immense responsibility for safety of human lives that is placed in the controllers hands it is essential that he does not have tendencies towards mental imbalance.

The total number of controllers in India is about 820, women form a percentage of just about 2.5, that is there are just about 20 controllers who are women.

An interesting point is that this profession is suitable only for the right handed. The arrangement of switches and display boards unconsciously assume that controllers are right handed for example the transmitting switches are all located to the left so that the controller can use his left hand to activate the switches and his right hand to 'mark' the flight progress strips or make jottings. Curiously there are hardly any controllers (in India) who are left handed. I know of only one controller who is left handed but who has somewhat managed to overcome what for this particular job, is a disability.

The total number of controllers in the entire world is also small in comparison to other professions. While I do not have the exact or even approximate figure in this regard, I believe that the total number of controllers would not exceed 300,000. The total area of the earth's surface is about 200 million square nautical miles. Assuming that only 2/3rd of this area has air traffic services coverage, the area within which air traffic services is provided will be about 130 square nautical miles. That is, just about three lakh controllers working in a huge network control air traffic by day and for most part by night also within an area of about 130 million square nautical miles.

Regarding the status and emoluments of controllers they were, at entry point equated to Group A officers of the central government and drew emoluments appropriate to that rank. The Airports Authority of India came into existence on 1st April 1995 and it has adopted it's own payscales. Controllers get extra allowances depending on the ratings they hold. However it appears that in the developed western nations controllers get a better deal than their counterparts in India even after discounting factors like general level of payscales, cost of living and so on.

Controllers have an unique professional relationship with pilots. The nature of the controllers job demands that he knows fully what is happening on the 'other side'. That is the controller must know how it is to be in the pilot's shoes. Logically therefore controllers should be given adequate opportunity to be on board in the cockpit to get a direct insight into the pilots problems so as to serve him better. A second reason for giving the controller the opportunity to fly on board an aircraft is that it will psychologically impress on his mind the enormity of the responsibility for safety of human lives that is placed in his hands. To a controller working in his unit, an aircraft is just an 'entry' on a flight progress strip or a speck of light on his radar screen. While flying on board an aircraft the fact mentally registers itself that the 'entry' or 'blip' is not an inanimate thing but one which carries human beings in various stages of life with various aspirations and expectations from life.

In spite of this, the controller gets only very limited chance to fly on board. With his emoluments he cannot afford to travel by air on his own. The 50% concession in airfares that Indian Airlines extends to Defence Officers is not given to a minuscule number of controllers. Realising that it is important for controllers to acquire familiarity with on-the-scene cockpit operation the Tata Committee on Civil Aviation which was set up for reorganisation of the Civil Aviation Department in the wake of the crash of an Indian Airlines aircraft in which a minister of the central cabinet met his unfortunate demise, recommended that airlines should extend 'familiarisation' flights to ATC officers. In implementation of this recommendation Indian Airlines grants such flights to controllers. This is however far short of the requirements. A controller may get a chance to fly once in three or four years. In the United States, in my talks with the ATC officers I was told that the controller gets eight domestic familiarisation flights and one international flight per year.

By virtue of being highly specialized, the controllers job has hardly any 'market' outside the government or the organisation designated for providing air traffic services in a country. The experience accumulated over the years by a controller has absolutely no'market value'. The controller has to work irregular hours, his job has no public 'visibility' (except of course when some untoward incident occurs). His life is one long cycle of 'afternoon duty, morning duty, night duty.' Days of the week cease to have any meaning to him. It is not unusual for a controller to go to a bank and finding it closed realise that 'today is Sunday'; or to pull up his son 'why are you not getting ready to go to school?' and to be told 'But, papa today is a holiday', In view of all these disabilities added to the strenous and tension ridden nature of the job, it is worth to join this profession only of the emoluments are good enough.

During the middle eighties many government departments were converted into autonomous units or corporations to free them from the shackles of government procedures so as to enable them to function effectively. The National Airports Authority was one such organisation that came into existence in 1986. Air Traffic Control which was under the Director General of Civil Aviation was transferred to that Authority. The National Airports Authority also assumed the functions of provision and maintenance of navigation and communication aids as well as passenger facilitation (i.e. construction and maintenance of passenger terminals and related amenities) the last only, in respect of domestic aerodromes.

With the formation of the National Airports Authority the senior officers of the Directorate-General of Civil Aviation who were inducted into that Authority were totally sidelined and rank outsiders were brought in as Members of the Board. The change from the staid government department to an autonomous body endowed with sweeping powers was abrupt. The new members showed little understanding of the controllers' problems, temperament or sentiments. Controllers are as a rule difficult people to deal with as a group. The nature of their job is perhaps responsible for this. They feel that they are working in a hostile environment where nobody appreciates them for work well done, but where the entire world is ready to pounce on them if something goes amiss. Moreover the younger generation of controllers were more demanding than their seniors. Consequently the relationship between the controllers and the administration deteriorated. Matters became worse, when the Authority in the name of rationalization of the administration of field aerodromes initiated in 1992 some measures, which the controllers perceived as totally inimical to their interests. They resisted by way of a 'work-to-rule'—the first time they had resorted to such action after a period of about a dozen years. The administration beat a hasty retreat. Matters again came to a head in 1996. A nearmiss had occurred at Delhi between two aircraft which were under radar control. The administration over reacted and ordered the concerned controller to be suspended. This provoked the entire ATC community to go on a lightening strike on 11 April 1996. As it happened that was the day the Deva Gowda government was fighting for its survival. Public attention was directed towards that and the controllers' strike therefore evoked lesser public attention than it normally would have. Still the effect was devastating. The government was taken aback. ("Who are these people? Never heard of them!" a top official of the Central Government is stated to have remarked). The authority gave in to the demands of the controllers and cancelled the suspension order. The effect of that one-day strike was felt for at least a couple of days at the airports of Southeast Asia where the aircraft had all been held up unable to operate their flights through the Indian Airspace.

In the wake of the strike the government set up a committee under chairmanship of Shri Bimal Jhulka of the Ministry of Civil Aviation to go into the demands of the controllers. The committee submitted its recommendations which were highly favourable to the controllers. When the ATC Guild pressed the administration to implement the recommendations, the Authority dithered. This led to another agitation by the controllers in November '97. The authority again gave in and enhanced the rating allowances of the controllers as per the committee's recommendations. Some other recommendations of the committee relating to duty allowance etc were not however accepted.

Bibliography

Chronicle of Aviation, Published by JL International Publishing 1992, Editor-in-chief Bul Gunston.

"Air Traffic Control", *The New Encyclopedia Britannica.* Volume 28, 15th edition, 1989.

"Navigation", *The New Encyclopedia Britannica*, Volume 24, 15th edition, 1989.

"Cospas Sarsat" Indian Space Research Organisation, December 1994.

A.S. Panneevselvam, "The bird has flown" *Outlook.* June 18, 1997.

"Boeing's Crisis in Bombay Skies, *The Times of India*, Bombay, June 30, 1989.

"Modernisation of Air Traffic Services", *Project Information Bulletin*, Airports Authority of India.

"Address by the President of the Council of the ICAO, Dr, Assad Kotaite" Global Navcom Synposium, Seattle, June 29, 1993.

"Twenty most frequently asked questions and some answers!", *The FANS CNS/ATM Implementation Starter Kit*, Section 4A, July 1994.

"Pilots Welcome Numerous Benefits offered by FANS", *ICAO Journal*, December 1991.

"Controllers Look Forward to Technology Enhancements", *ICAO Journal*, December 1991.

Index